Childcraft
THE HOW AND WHY LIBRARY

VOLUME 9

Holidays and Birthdays

World Book, Inc.

a Scott Fetzer company

Chicago London Sydney Toronto

World Book, Inc.
525 W. Monroe
Chicago, IL 60661

© 1994, 1993, 1991, 1990, 1989, 1987, 1986, 1985 by World Book,
Inc. © 1982, 1981, 1980, 1979 U.S.A. by World Book-Childcraft
International, Inc. © 1976, 1974, 1973, 1971, 1970, 1969, 1968, 1965,
1964 U.S.A. by Field Enterprises Educational Corporation.
International Copyright © 1987, 1986, 1985 by World Book, Inc.
International Copyright © 1982, 1981, 1980, 1979 by World Book-
Childcraft International, Inc.
International Copyright © 1976, 1974, 1973, 1971, 1970, 1969, 1968,
1965, 1964 by Field Enterprises Educational Corporation.

ISBN 0-7166-0195-8
Library of Congress Catalog Card Number 94-60730
Printed in the United States of America
  2 3 4 5 6 7 8 9 10 99 98 97 96 95 94

Acknowledgments

The publishers of Childcraft—The How and Why Library
gratefully acknowledge the courtesy of the following
publishers, agencies, authors, individuals, and organizations
for permission to use copyrighted stories and poems in this
volume. Full illustration acknowledgments appear on pages
328-329.

Frances Dimity: First stanza of "The Flag Goes By" by
Henry Holcomb Bennett reprinted with the permission of
Frances van Swearingen Bennett Dimity.

Grosset & Dunlap, Inc.: "The Sugar Egg" by Carolyn
Sherwin Bailey. Reprinted from Merry Tales for Children,
copyright © 1941 by Milton Bradley Company, copyright ©
1943 by The Platt & Munk Co., Inc. Used by permission of
Grosset & Dunlap, Inc.

Harper & Row, Publishers, Inc.: A text excerpt from Farmer
Boy by Laura Ingalls Wilder, copyright © 1933, as to text,
by Harper & Row, Publishers, Inc. Renewed © 1961 by
Roger L. MacBride. By permission of Harper & Row,
Publishers, Inc., and Lutterworth Press.

Hebrew Publishing Company: Potato Pancakes All Around
by Marilyn Hirsh, copyright © 1978 by Marilyn Hirsh.
Reprinted by permission of Hebrew Publishing Company.

William Morrow & Company, Inc.: Adaptation and
abridgment of My Mother Is the Most Beautiful Woman in
the World by Becky Reyher (without illustrations). Copyright
1945, renewed © 1973 by Becky Reyher and Ruth
Gannett. By permission of Lothrop, Lee & Shepard (a
division of William Morrow & Company) and McIntosh &
Otis, Inc.

G. P. Putnam's Sons: First stanza of "In Flanders Fields"
from In Flanders Fields and Other Poems by John McCrae.
Copyright © 1919, 1946, by G. P. Putnam's Sons.
Reprinted by permission of G. P. Putnam's Sons and
Hodder & Stoughton, Ltd.

Charles Scribner's Sons: "New Year's Hats for the Statues"
by Yoshiko Uchida from The Sea of Gold and Other Tales
from Japan is used by permission of Charles Scribner's
Sons. Copyright © 1965 by Yoshiko Uchida.

Union of American Hebrew Congregations: "Dreidel Song"
from Now We Begin by Marian J. and Efraim M.
Rosenzweig. Published by Union of American Hebrew
Congregations. Reprinted by permission.

The Viking Press: "The Peddler of Ballaghaderreen" from
The Way of the Storyteller by Ruth Sawyer. Copyright 1942
by Ruth Sawyer, © renewed 1970 by Ruth Sawyer.
Reprinted by permission of Viking Penguin Inc.

Volume 9

Holidays and Birthdays

Contents

5

Holiday Time

All kinds of holidays

Hurray, it's a holiday!

Many holidays are days when you don't
have to go to school and grown-ups don't
have to go to work. These are often fun-filled
days when your family gets together for a
big dinner, a picnic, or a backyard barbecue.
Sometimes there are parades or fireworks.
And on some holidays people go to a church
or other house of worship. The very word
holiday means "holy day"—a day on which
people thank or honor God.

We celebrate all kinds of holidays. Many,
such as Christmas, Yom Kippur, and others
are religious holidays, or holy days. Some

holidays are the birthdays of great leaders or of famous people, such as Benito Juárez and George Washington. Others, such as Bastille Day in France, are the birthdays of nations. And there are a number of special days, such as Remembrance Day in Canada. These holidays remind us of those who have helped their country in time of war.

We also celebrate traditional holidays, one of which is Thanksgiving. There are also holidays for special groups of people. Labor Day is one of these. It is a holiday in honor of working people. And in Japan there is Children's Day—a special day in honor of children.

Holidays and calendars

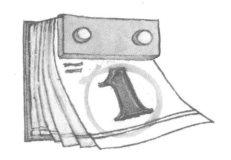

The first holidays were holy days. In fact, the word *holiday* comes from an Old English word, *haligdaeg*, which means "holy day."

Many of our holidays today are holy days. But we also celebrate many other kinds of holidays. Why, you even celebrate a holiday that is yours alone. Do you know what it is?

When you want to know what day a holiday falls on, you look at a calendar. Long ago, the only "calendars" people had were the moon, sun, stars, and seasons. Even today we still use "moon calendars" and "sun calendars." Do you know which kind you use?

Have you ever *really* thought about the days of the week and the months of the year? How do you think they got their names? Do you know what the names mean?

You will find out about all of these things—and many others—as you read this book. So, good reading—and have a happy holiday!

Every day's a holiday

Every day of the year there is a holiday somewhere. Often, there are many different holidays on the same day. If you wanted to, you could celebrate all year long. Here, for example, are a few of the holidays that come on the first seven days of March.

March 1 is a traditional spring holiday in the Engadine Valley in Switzerland. On this day, young people in costumes ring bells and crack whips to drive away the demons of winter.

It was on March 2, 1836, that Texas declared its independence from Mexico. And Sam Houston, one of the people who led the Texans in their fight for freedom, was born on this day in 1793. So, this is a double holiday in Texas.

March 3 is a national holiday in Morocco, a country in North Africa. Morocco is ruled by a king, and this day is celebrated as the Anniversary of the Throne.

On March 4, 1791, Vermont became the fourteenth state of the United States. So, the people of Vermont celebrate March 4 as Admission Day.

On March 5, Massachusetts remembers what has come to be called the Boston Massacre. On this day in 1770, several colonists were killed in a street fight with British soldiers. One of the people killed was Crispus Attucks, who may have been a

King Hassan II of Morocco

runaway slave. His death is remembered in New Jersey, where this is Crispus Attucks Day.

March 6 is Independence Day in the African country of Ghana. And on the little Pacific island of Guam, nearly halfway around the world, March 6 is known as Magellan Day. It was on this day in 1521 that the Portuguese explorer Ferdinand Magellan landed on the island.

March 7 is the birthday of Luther Burbank. This great naturalist, who was born in 1849, developed many new trees and flowers. In California, where he lived for many years, his birthday is celebrated as Conservation, Bird, and Arbor Day.

Luther Burbank

Your very own holiday

You have a holiday that is your very own—your birthday!

The day you were born is a very special day for you and your family. You probably celebrate this holiday with a birthday cake, perhaps with a party—and by getting presents!

For thousands of years, people all over the world have thought of a birthday as a very special day. Long ago, people believed that on a birthday a person could be helped by good spirits or hurt by evil spirits. So, when a person had a birthday, friends and relatives gathered to protect him or her. And that's how birthday parties began.

The idea of putting candles on birthday cakes goes back to ancient Greece. The

Greeks worshipped many gods and goddesses.
Among them was one called Artemis (AHR tuh
mihs).

Artemis was the goddess of the moon. The
Greeks celebrated her birthday once each
month by bringing special cakes to her
temple. The cakes were round, like a full
moon. And, because the moon glows with
light, the cakes were decorated with lighted
candles.

Not all people celebrate their birthdays.
Some people celebrate their name days
instead. In certain religions, children are
named for saints. Each saint is honored on a
special day, called the saint's feast day.
People who are named for saints often
celebrate the saints' feast days, or their name
days, rather than their own birthdays.

At the front of each of the following
sections of this book there is a birthday
calendar for the month. It will tell you what
famous person shares your birthday.

Birthday symbols

Did you know that each month has a special jewel (called a birthstone), a special flower, and a special color?

Here are the months and their special symbols. Find the month you were born in. What is your birthstone and what is it supposed to mean? What is your lucky flower? And what is supposed to be your favorite color?

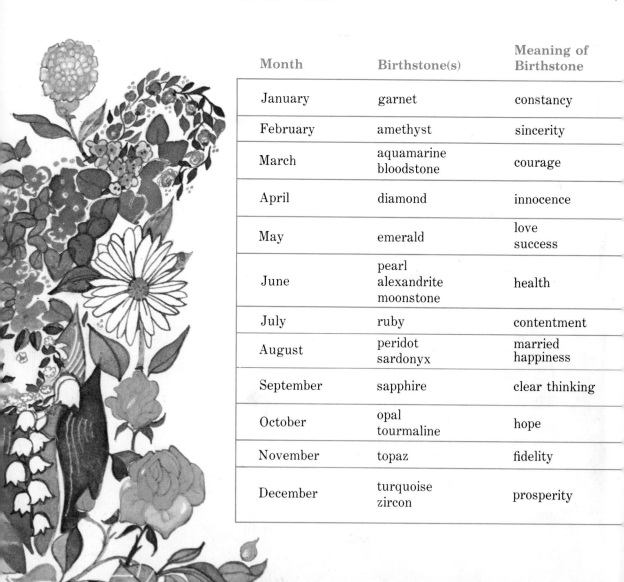

Month	Birthstone(s)	Meaning of Birthstone
January	garnet	constancy
February	amethyst	sincerity
March	aquamarine bloodstone	courage
April	diamond	innocence
May	emerald	love success
June	pearl alexandrite moonstone	health
July	ruby	contentment
August	peridot sardonyx	married happiness
September	sapphire	clear thinking
October	opal tourmaline	hope
November	topaz	fidelity
December	turquoise zircon	prosperity

Flower(s)	Color(s)
snowdrop carnation	black white
primrose	deep blue
violet	silver
sweet pea daisy	yellow
hawthorn lily of the valley	lavender lilac
rose	pink rose
water lily	sky blue
poppy gladiolus	deep green
morning-glory	orange gold
calendula	brown
chrysanthemum	purple
holly narcissus poinsettia	red

Happy anniversary!

Married people have their own special holidays, called wedding anniversaries. This is when they celebrate the number of years they have been married.

People often give gifts made of a certain kind of material to a man and a woman who have been married a certain number of years. The wedding anniversary is called by the name of the material. So, if your parents are celebrating their tenth wedding anniversary, this will be their "tin anniversary."

Here are the kinds of gifts given for certain wedding anniversaries:

Anniversary	Gift
first	paper
second	cotton
third	leather
fourth	linen, silk, or rayon
fifth	wood
sixth	iron
seventh	wool
eighth	bronze
ninth	china
tenth	tin
twenty-fifth	silver
fiftieth	gold
seventy-fifth	diamond

Seven days make a week

Monday's child is fair of face,
Tuesday's child is full of grace,
Wednesday's child is full of woe,
Thursday's child has far to go,
Friday's child is loving and giving,
Saturday's child works hard for his living,
And the child that is born on the Sabbath day
Is bonny and blithe and good and gay.

Old Nursery Rhyme

Why are there seven days in a week? Why not six, eight, or ten?

The word *week* means "a turning." Long ago, a week was the length of time between market days. This was anywhere from four to ten days.

We don't know for certain why or when the seven-day week began. The idea may have come from the people of ancient Babylon. Among them, the number seven was sacred. They also worshiped the seven heavenly bodies that they could see—the moon, the sun, and five of the planets—Mercury, Venus, Mars, Jupiter, and Saturn.

We do know that the ancient Hebrews were among the first people to adopt a seven-day week. Their week was based on the story of Creation in the Bible. There, it says that God created the world in six days and rested on the seventh.

Have you ever wondered about the names of the days and what they mean? Here are the stories behind the names of the days.

17

Sunday is the first day of the week. It is named for the sun. The Romans called this day *dies solis*, or "day of the sun." Long ago, people called Anglo-Saxons lived in England. Their name for this day was *sunnandaeg*, or "sun's day." In time, this became Sunday. The early Christians made this day their Sabbath, or day of rest and worship, because Christ rose from the dead on a Sunday.

Monday is the second day of the week. It is named for the moon. The Roman name for this day was *dies lunae*, or "day of the moon." The Anglo-Saxons called it *monandaeg* or "moon's day." In time, this became Monday.

Thursday is the fifth day of the week. It is named for Thor, the Norse god of thunder. The Romans called this day *dies Jovis*, or "Jove's day," after Jove (Jupiter), their chief god. The Anglo-Saxons named this day *Thuresdaeg*, or "Thor's day." In time, this became Thursday.

Wednesday is the fourth day of the week. It is named for Woden (Odin), who was the most powerful of the Norse gods. The Roman name for this day was *dies Mercurii*, or "Mercury's day." Mercury was the swift messenger of the gods. The Anglo-Saxons called this day *Wodnesdaeg*, or "Woden's day." In time, this became Wednesday. But we say WEHNZ dee, or WEHNZ day, because this is easier than WEHD nehs day.

18

Tuesday is the third day of the week. It is named for Tyr, the Norse god of war. The Romans called this day *dies Martis*, or "Mar's day," after their god of war. The Anglo-Saxons called it *Tiwesdaeg*, or "Tiw's (Tyr's) day." In time, this became Tuesday.

Friday is the sixth day of the week. It is named for Frigg, the Norse goddess of love. The Romans called this day *dies Veneris*, or "Venus's day," after their goddess of love. The Anglo-Saxons called it *Frigedaeg*, or "Frigg's day." Now we call it Friday.

Saturday is the seventh day of the week. It is named for Saturn, the Roman god of farming. The Roman name for this day was *dies Saturni*, or "Saturn's day." Among the Anglo-Saxons this became *Saeterdaeg*. And now it is Saturday. The Jews made this day their Sabbath, or day of rest and worship, because the Bible says that God created the world in six days and rested on the seventh.

19

March
June
February
April
May
January

Twelve months make a year

Thirty days hath September,
April, June, and November;
All the rest have thirty-one,
Except February alone,
And that has twenty-eight days clear
And twenty-nine in each leap year.

Old Nursery Rhyme

What is a month? Why do we have twelve
months in a year? And why doesn't each
month have the same number of days?

Our word *month* comes from the Old
English word *monath*. And *monath* comes
from *mona*, which means "moon." So, a
month is a "moon."

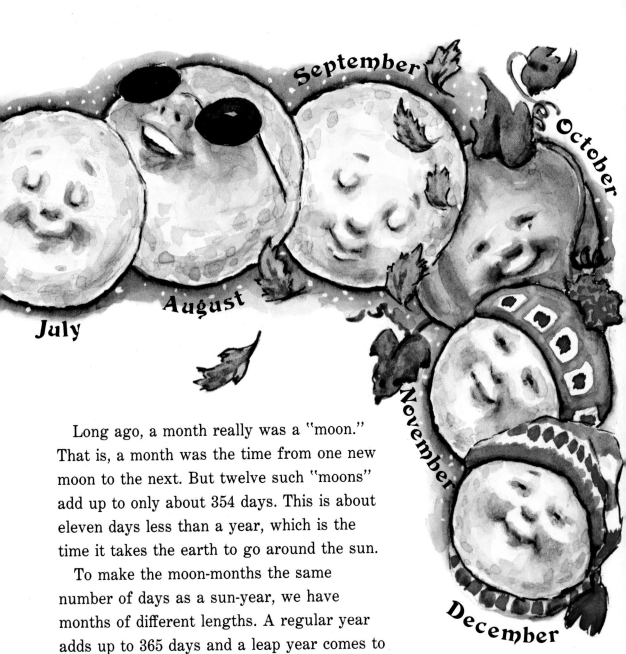

July

August

September

October

November

December

Long ago, a month really was a "moon." That is, a month was the time from one new moon to the next. But twelve such "moons" add up to only about 354 days. This is about eleven days less than a year, which is the time it takes the earth to go around the sun.

To make the moon-months the same number of days as a sun-year, we have months of different lengths. A regular year adds up to 365 days and a leap year comes to 366 days. In this way, the months keep time with the seasons.

The rest of this book is divided into twelve sections—one for each month. At the front of each section you will discover how the month got its name, what the name means, and other interesting facts about that month.

When does a year begin?

For most people, the first day of the year is January 1. But this was not always so. The ancient Greeks started their year on the first day of winter—December 21 or 22. The Romans began their year on March 1. Then they changed the calendar and moved the start of the year to January 1.

Many other countries also used January 1. But some went back to March 1, and others chose September 1. At one time, some Christian countries made December 25, Christmas, the first day of the year. And, about a thousand years ago, many nations switched to March 25.

At one time, a French king made Easter the first of the year. Another time, about two hundred years ago, the French moved the start of the year to September 22.

Even today, many people celebrate the first of the year on different dates. The Jewish New Year is on Tishri 1, between September 5 and October 5. And in the Russian Orthodox Church, the year starts on January 14.

In Iran, the new year begins on March 21. The Iranians call this *No Ruz*, which means "New Day." And many Chinese living outside China celebrate the old Chinese New Year. It falls between January 21 and February 19.

There is nothing special about January 1. It really doesn't matter when a year begins.

23

The changing calendar

People made the first calendars by dividing a year into twelve "moons," or months. But they had a problem. A year is the time it takes the earth to travel once around the sun. This comes to about 365¼ days. A moon-month is the time from one new moon to the next. This is about 29½ days. So twelve "moons" come to about 354 days. And this is eleven days *less* than a year.

Sometimes people added days or months to keep the calendar in step with the seasons. And sometimes they paid no attention. The early Romans had a ten-month calendar. The year, which began in March and ended in December, was only 304 days long. They just ignored the other days.

Later, to make a better calendar, the Romans added two more months. Even so, when the great Roman leader Julius Caesar came to power, the calendar was out of step with the seasons by 90 days. Caesar had a

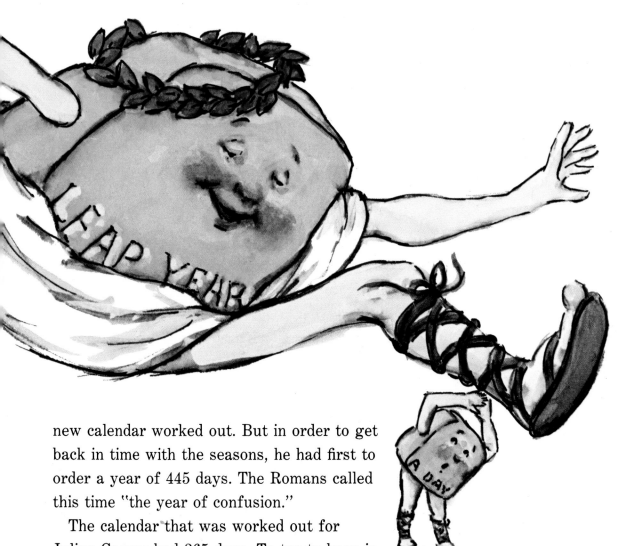

new calendar worked out. But in order to get back in time with the seasons, he had first to order a year of 445 days. The Romans called this time "the year of confusion."

The calendar that was worked out for Julius Caesar had 365 days. To try to keep in time with the seasons, an extra day was added every four years. We still do this today. The year with the extra day is called leap year.

Why is it called "leap year"? It's because in a leap year, the calendar "leaps over" one day. In the regular years, a fixed holiday, such as July 4, comes *one* day later each year. But in a leap year, there is an extra day in February. As a result, all fixed holidays after February fall *two* days later than in the year before. The calendar has "leaped over" one day.

The Julian calendar, as it came to be called, worked quite well. But it was a little more than eleven minutes longer than an average year. By about four hundred years ago, this little error had added up to ten days!

In 1582, Pope Gregory XIII ordered that the error be fixed. So, October 5 of that year became October 15. To keep the same thing from happening again, it was decided that not all century years—1600, 1700, and so on—would be leap years. Only the ones that could be divided by four hundred would be leap years.

Because of religious problems, the new calendar—now called the Gregorian calendar—wasn't accepted by all countries. For hundreds of years, some countries continued to use the old Julian calendar. But today almost all countries use the Gregorian calendar for day-to-day business purposes.

When you see a date such as 1989, what does the number mean? When you see a date such as 46 B.C. or A.D. 500, what do the letters mean?

The calendar we use today counts years *after* the birth of Christ. So, 1989 means 1,989 years after Christ's birth. The letters B.C. stand for Before Christ. So, 46 B.C. means 46 years before the birth of Christ.

The letters A.D. stand for *anno Domini*, which means "in the year of our Lord." This abbreviation is used with dates after the birth of Christ. A.D. 500 means 500 years after the birth of Christ.

Different calendars

The calendar you use every day isn't the only kind of calendar. There are others.

The Hebrew, or Jewish, calendar is used to fix the dates of the Jewish religious year. It follows both the moon and the sun. There are twelve months, based on the moon. A thirteenth month, added seven times every nineteen years, keeps the calendar more or less in time with the seasons. Also, days are added or taken away to make sure certain holy days do not fall on certain days of the week. As a result, a Jewish year can be as short as 353 days or as long as 385 days.

Hebrew Calendar

Month	Days
1. Tishri	30
2. Heshvan	29
3. Kislev	30
4. Tebet	29
5. Shebat	30
6. Adar	29
7. Nisan	30
8. Iyar	29
9. Sivan	30
10. Tammuz	29
11. Ab	30
12. Elul	29
	354

Seven times in every nineteen years, an extra month, Veadar, is put in between Adar and Nisan. This month has 29 days. At the same time, Adar is given an extra day.

Islamic Calendar

Month	Days
1. Muharram	30
2. Safar	29
3. Rabi I	30
4. Rabi II	29
5. Jumada I	30
6. Jumada II	29
7. Rajab	30
8. Shaban	29
9. Ramadan	30
10. Shawwal	29
11. Zulkadah	30
12. Zulhijjah	29
	354

The Islamic calendar is divided into thirty-year periods. In each period of thirty years, eleven of the years have one extra day. This extra day is added to Zulhijjah.

According to tradition, the Hebrew calendar started at the time of Creation—3,760 years before the birth of Christ. Thus 1980 was the year 5740 on the Hebrew calendar. It doesn't work out to the exact month because the Jewish year begins in September or October, not in January.

Muslims—people who follow the Islamic religion—use a calendar based on the moon. It has twelve months of 30 or 29 days. Eleven times every thirty years, an extra day is added. This keeps the calendar in time with the moon, but not with the seasons.

Because the Islamic year is only 354 or 355 days long, holidays move backward through the seasons. Each year, a holiday comes about eleven days sooner. But in thirty-three years it is back where it started.

The year 1 on the Islamic calendar was the year 622 on the Gregorian calendar. Thus 1980 was the year 1400 on the Islamic calendar.

The Chinese calendar, which also follows the moon, divides the years into groups of twelve. Each year is named for an animal. The first of the twelve years is the Year of the Rat. This is followed by the Ox, Tiger, Hare, Dragon, Snake, Horse, Sheep, Monkey, Rooster, Dog, and Pig. On the Chinese calendar, 1980 was the Year of the Monkey.

Christian Churches also use the moon to set some holy days. Easter, for example, can fall any time from March 22 through April 25. The exact date depends on the moon.

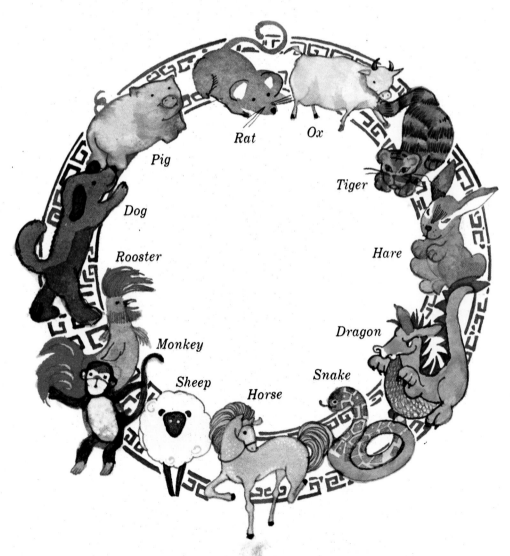

Rat

Ox

Pig

Tiger

Dog

Rooster

Hare

Dragon

Monkey

Snake

Sheep

Horse

January

1

Paul Revere (1735) hero of the American Revolution

Betsy Ross (1752) flag maker in the American Revolution

2

James Wolfe (1727) British general who won Canada for Great Britain

Isaac Asimov (1920) American biochemist and author

3

Lucretia Mott (1793) American Quaker and women's rights leader

J. R. R. Tolkien (1892) British author of *The Hobbit* and *The Lord of the Rings*

4

Jakob Grimm (1785) German collector of fairy tales

Louis Braille (1809) French inventor of a system of writing for the blind

Who shares my birthday?

Is your birthday in January? The names of some of the famous people born in January are shown on the calendar on this page and the next. What do you know about the person who shares your birthday?

5

Stephen Decatur (1779) American naval hero in the War of 1812

Zebulon Pike (1779) American explorer for whom Pikes Peak was named

6

Joan of Arc (1412) French heroine who led the French army to victory

Carl Sandburg (1878) American poet and biographer of Abraham Lincoln

7

Millard Fillmore (1800) 13th President of the United States

Bernadette Soubirous (1844) French saint from Lourdes

8

Gerald Durrell (1925) British naturalist and author

Elvis Presley (1935) American rock music singer and motion-picture star

9

Carrie Chapman Catt (1859) American leader in women's right to vote

Richard M. Nixon (1913) 37th President of the United States

10

Robinson Jeffers (1887) American poet

Ray Bolger (1904) American entertainer; played the scarecrow in *The Wizard of Oz*

11

Alice Paul (1885) American leader in fight for equal rights for women

James Earl Jones (1931) American motion-picture actor

12

Charles Perrault (1628) French writer of fairy tales

Jack London (1876) American author who wrote *The Call of the Wild*

13

Salmon P. Chase (1808) antislavery leader

Francis Everett Townsend (1867) American physician and social reformer

14

Albert Schweitzer (1875) German doctor and missionary

Hugh Lofting (1886) English author who wrote the Doctor Dolittle books

15

Horatio Alger (1832) American author of boys' books

Martin Luther King, Jr. (1929) American minister and civil rights leader

16

Robert W. Service
(1874) Canadian
"Poet of the Yukon"

**Jerome (Dizzy)
Dean** (1911)
American baseball
player and
sportscaster

17

Benjamin Franklin
(1706) American
statesman and
inventor

Mack Sennett
(1880) Canadian
film producer

18

A. A. Milne
(1882) English
author who wrote
Winnie-the-Pooh

Muhammad Ali
(1942) American
heavyweight boxing
champion

19

Robert E. Lee
(1807) Confederate
army commander

Oveta Culp Hobby
(1905) first U.S.
secretary of health,
education, and
welfare

20

Harold Gray (1894)
American cartoonist
who created "Little
Orphan Annie"

Joy Adamson
(1920) British author
of *Born Free*

21

Ethan Allen (1738)
hero of the American
Revolution; captured
Fort Ticonderoga

**Thomas
"Stonewall"
Jackson** (1824)
Confederate general

22

Lord Byron (1788)
English poet

U Thant (1909)
Burmese diplomat

23

John Hancock
(1737) first signer of
the U.S. Declaration
of Independence

24

Edith Wharton
(1862) American
writer

Maria Tallchief
(1925) American
ballet star

25

Robert Burns
(1759) Scottish poet

Edwin Newman
(1919) American
newsman

26

**Mary Mapes
Dodge** (1831)
American author who
wrote *Hans Brinker*

Maria (von) Trapp
(1905) Austrian
leader of the Trapp
Family Singers

27

**Wolfgang Amadeus
Mozart** (1756)
Austrian composer

Lewis Carroll (1832)
English author of
*Alice's Adventures
in Wonderland*

28

Henry VII (1457)
first English king of
the House of Tudor

**Sir Henry Morton
Stanley** (1841)
Anglo-American
explorer

29

Thomas Paine
(1737) writer in the
American Revolution

William McKinley
(1843) 25th President
of the United States

30

Franklin Roosevelt
(1882) 32nd President
of the United States

Eleanor C. Smeal
(1930) American
feminist

31

Zane Grey (1872)
American author of
Old West novels

Jackie Robinson
(1919) first black
player in modern
major league baseball

The month of Janus

In most of the world, January is the first month of the year. Named for the Roman god Janus, January has thirty-one days.

Long ago, the Romans had only ten months in their year. Then they added an eleventh month. They called this month *Januarius*, in honor of the Roman god Janus. Later, the Romans made *Januarius* the first month. They thought this fitting, because Janus was a very important god.

Janus was the god of beginnings and the god of gates and doorways. He is shown with two faces. One face looks to the future. The other face looks back upon the past.

Among people living in England long ago, this month was known as *Wulf-monath*, or "Wolf month." This was the time of year when hungry wolves often entered villages.

In the northern part of the world, January is cold and snowy. It is the beginning of winter. People go skating and sledding. But in the southern part of the world, January is warm. It is the beginning of summer, and a time for swimming and picnics.

Ring in the new!

Ring out wild bells to the wild sky,
    The flying cloud, the frosty light;
    The year is dying in the night;
Ring out, wild bells, and let him die.

Ring out the old, ring in the new,
    Ring happy bells, across the snow;
    The year is going, let him go;
Ring out the false, ring in the true.

from *In Memoriam*
by Alfred Tennyson

Shhhh! It's only seconds till midnight. The old year is dying. The new year is almost here. As the clock begins to strike twelve, noise fills the air. Church bells ring; people toot horns and blow whistles. Everyone shouts, "Happy New Year!"

Why all the noise? It's one way people show how happy they are. It's also an old custom. Long ago, people believed that loud noises scared away evil spirits. Maybe they do. Maybe they don't. But one good thing about New Year's Eve—you get to stay up a lot later than usual.

If you live in Scotland, you'll be able to stay up to welcome the first person to enter your house after midnight. This person is called the "first-footer." People believe that if the first-footer is a dark-haired man, the family will have good luck in the new year.

First-footing is part of the old Scottish New Year's Eve celebration called Hogmanay (HAHG muh nay). It is a time for old friends and relatives to get together—and to end up singing "Auld Lang Syne." *Auld lang syne* is Scottish for "old long since," or simply "days gone by."

You may not live in Scotland. But wherever you live, everyone wishes you good luck—and a happy new year!

Happy New Year!

The first day of the year is both a holiday and a holy day. It is also a time to look back and a time to look ahead. It is a time to make a new beginning. So, many people make New Year's resolutions. They promise themselves to do better in the new year than they did in the old year.

Because New Year's Day is a Christian holy day, many people begin the day by going

The giant figures for the floats in the New Year's Day Rose Parade are made of chicken wire that is covered with papier-mâché. They are then decorated with hundreds of roses.

to church. But it is also a day to visit friends and relatives and to exchange gifts.

In the United States, parades and college football games are the big events of the day. Millions of people across the country watch both on television. In Pasadena, California, there is the Tournament of Roses. Festivities begin with a parade of colorful floats and marching bands. After the parade comes the Rose Bowl football game.

There are also parades and football games at the Cotton Bowl in Dallas, Texas, at the

Each Rose parade has a theme. The theme of this parade was "Thanks to Communications." This float shows how aliens might try to communicate with people on earth.

Sugar Bowl in New Orleans, Louisiana, and at the Orange Bowl in Miami, Florida.

People near Philadelphia, Pennsylvania, flock to see something quite different—the Mummers' Parade. A mummer is a person who wears a mask, a fancy costume, or a disguise for fun. Every year, thousands of people in strange costumes take part in the parade. Of course, there are prizes for the best costumes.

In Russia, children who live in the city of Moscow may visit the Kremlin Palace of Congresses. There they will see a huge fir tree called the New Year Tree. The tree is decorated with countless colored lights. The children may also see a fairy-tale play and get gifts from Grandfather Frost and his helper the Snow Maiden.

People in Sweden attend church services in the morning. Then comes a big family dinner, much like the one at Christmas. They will enjoy tempting foods and a hot spiced wine called glogg (gluhg).

In many parts of the world, people have special foods that are supposed to bring good luck in the coming year. In Japan, it's a kind of fish called red snapper. This fish has a pink color. In Japan, pink is considered lucky.

Families in Greece share a New Year's cake called *peta*. A coin is baked inside the cake. Whoever gets the coin is supposed to have good luck for a whole year. In other countries in Europe, roast pig is often served on New Year's Day. Usually the pig has an apple or

In Russia, Grandfather Frost and his helper the Snow Maiden give New Year's gifts to children.

an orange in its mouth. But in Hungary, it is a four-leaf clover—for good luck.

In the south of India, the food that brings good luck is boiled new rice. And in the Southern and Southwestern United States, many people enjoy black-eyed peas so as to have good luck throughout the year.

In many countries, gifts are exchanged on New Year's Day instead of on Christmas. Long ago, in England, husbands used to give their wives money on New Year's Day. The money was to buy pins for the whole year. At that time, pins were made by hand and were expensive. After machines were developed to make cheap pins, the custom disappeared. But we still use the expression "pin money," meaning a small amount of money for one's own use.

In Japan, houses are decorated with rice cakes and sprays of sweet-smelling pine. The Japanese believe that they should begin the new year without owing money to anyone.

New Year's Day has been celebrated for more than five thousand years—but not always on January 1 (see page 22). Even today, people in many parts of the world begin their new year on other dates.

Jews celebrate their new year, Rosh Ha-Shanah, in September or October. The Chinese new year begins in January or February. And for the people who follow the Islamic religion, the new year starts on the first day of their first month, called Muharram.

New Year's punch

This tasty punch is easy to make. The directions will make enough for about twenty cupfuls.

2 quarts (1.9 liters) of
   ginger ale, chilled
6 scoops of raspberry
   or orange sherbet
1 unpeeled orange,
   cut in thin slices
10 ice cubes
large punch bowl
punch cups
bottle opener

Pour the ginger ale into the punch bowl. Add the sherbet. Break up each scoopful so it will melt. Put in the ice cubes and stir. Add orange slices for decoration. Pour the punch into cups and serve. Happy New Year!

New Year's Hats for the Statues

by Yoshiko Uchida

Once a very kind old man and woman lived
in a small house high in the hills of Japan.
Although they were good people, they were
very, very poor, for the old man made his
living by weaving the reed hats that farmers
used to ward off the sun and rain, and even
in a year's time, he could not sell very many.

One cold winter day as the year was drawing to an end, the old woman said to the old man, "Good husband, it will soon be New Year's Day, but we have nothing in the house to eat. How will we welcome the new year without even a pot of fresh rice?" A worried frown hovered over her face, and she sighed sadly as she looked into her empty cupboards.

But the old man patted her shoulders and said, "Now, now, don't you worry. I will make some reed hats and take them to the village to sell. Then with the money I earn I will buy some fish and rice for our New Year's feast."

On the day before New Year's, the old man set out for the village with five new reed hats that he had made. It was bitterly cold, and from early morning,, snow tumbled from the skies and blew in great drifts about their small house. The old man shivered in the wind, but he thought about the fresh warm rice and the fish turning crisp and brown over the charcoal, and he knew he must earn some money to buy them. He pulled his wool scarf tighter about his throat and plodded on slowly over the snow-covered roads.

When he got to the village, he trudged up and down its narrow streets calling, "Reed hats for sale! Reed hats for sale!" But everyone was too busy preparing for the new year to be bothered with reed hats. They scurried by him, going instead to the shops where they could buy sea bream and red beans and herring roe for their New Year's feasts. No one even bothered to look at the old man or his hats.

As the old man wandered about the village, the snow fell faster, and before long the sky began to grow dark. The old man knew it was useless to linger, and he sighed with longing as he passed the fish shop and saw the rows of fresh fish.

"If only I could bring home one small piece of fish for my wife," he thought glumly, but his pockets were even emptier than his stomach.

There was nothing to do but to go home again with his five unsold hats. The old man headed wearily back toward his little house in the hills, bending his head against the biting cold of the wind. As he walked along, he came upon six stone statues of Jizo, the guardian god of children. They stood by the roadside covered with snow that had piled in small drifts on top of their heads and shoulders.

"Mah, mah, you are covered with snow," the old man said to the statues, and setting down his bundle, he stopped to brush the snow from their heads. As he was about to go on, a fine idea occurred to him.

"I am sorry these are only reed hats I could not sell," he apologized, "but at least they will keep the snow off your heads." And carefully he tied one on each of the Jizo statues.

"Now if I had one more there would be enough for each of them," he murmured as he looked at the row of statues. But the old man did not hesitate for long. Quickly he took the hat from his own head and tied it on the head of the sixth statue.

"There," he said looking pleased. "Now all of you are covered." Then, bowing in farewell, he told the statues that he must be going. "A happy new year to each of you," he called, and he hurried away content.

When he got home the old woman was waiting anxiously for him. "Did you sell your hats?" she asked. "Were you able to buy some rice and fish?"

The old man shook his head. "I couldn't sell a single hat," he explained, "but I did find a very good use for them." And he told her how he had put them on the Jizo statues that stood in the snow.

"Ah, that was a very kind thing to do," the old woman said. "I would have done exactly the same." And she did not complain at all that the old man had not brought home anything to eat. Instead she made some hot tea and added a precious piece of charcoal to the brazier so the old man could warm himself.

That night they went to bed early, for there was no more charcoal and the house had grown cold. Outside the wind continued to blow the snow in a white curtain that wrapped itself about the small house. The old man and woman huddled beneath their thick quilts and tried to keep warm.

"We are fortunate to have a roof over our heads on such a night," the old man said.

"Indeed we are," the old woman agreed, and before long they were both fast asleep.

About daybreak, when the sky was still a misty gray, the old man awakened for he heard voices outside.

"Listen," he whispered to the old woman.

"What is it? What is it?" the old woman asked.

Together they held their breath and listened. It sounded like a group of men pulling a very heavy load.

"*Yoi-sah! Hoi-sah! Yoi-sah! Hoi-sah!*" the voices called and seemed to come closer and closer.

"Who could it be so early in the morning?"

the old man wondered. Soon, they heard the
men singing.

"Where is the home of the kind old man,
The man who covered our heads?
Where is the home of the kind old man,
Who gave us hats for our heads?"

The old man and woman hurried to the
window to look out, and there in the snow
they saw the six stone Jizo statues lumbering
toward their house. They still wore the reed
hats the old man had given them and each
one was pulling a heavy sack.

"*Yoi-sah! Hoi-sah! Yoi-sah! Hoi-sah!*" they
called as they drew nearer and nearer.

"They seem to be coming here!" the old
man gasped in amazement. But the old
woman was too surprised even to speak.

As they watched, each of the Jizo statues
came up to their house and left his sack at
the doorstep.

The old man hurried to open the door, and as he did, the six big sacks came tumbling inside. In the sacks the old man and woman found rice and wheat, fish and beans, wine and bean paste cakes, and all sorts of delicious things that they might want to eat.

"Why, there is enough here for a feast every day all during the year!" the old man cried excitedly.

"And we shall have the finest New Year's feast we have ever had in our lives," the old woman exclaimed.

"Ojizo Sama, thank you!" the old man shouted.

"Ojizo Sama, how can we thank you enough?" the old woman called out.

But the six stone statues were already moving slowly down the road, and as the old man and woman watched, they disappeared into the whiteness of the falling snow, leaving only their footprints to show that they had been there at all.

The gift of the Magi

On the night of January 5, children in Puerto Rico look forward to a visit from the Three Kings.

It is said that the Three Kings, also called the Three Wise Men, or Magi, were named Gaspar (GAS puhr), Melchior (MEHL kee awr), and Balthasar (bal THAY zuhr). They followed a guiding star to a stable in Bethlehem. There, they gave the Christ Child gifts of gold, frankincense (FRANG kihn sehns), and myrrh (mur).

With this story in mind, just before bedtime the children fill their shoes with grass or straw. It's for the animals the Three Kings rode on their journey. The next morning, which is Three Kings' Day, the children find candy and toys in their shoes—gifts from the Three Kings.

In Italy, the night of January 5 is also an exciting time. All the children look forward

In Italy, it is the kind old witch Befana who brings presents to children. But today, Babbo Natale, *or Father Christmas, is also very popular.*

eagerly to a visit from Befana. Befana was a kind old witch who was too busy cleaning house to join the Three Kings on their journey. Ever since, Befana has looked for the Christ Child. In her search, she leaves candy and gifts for the children. They will find her gifts the next day—the Feast of the Epiphany (ih PIHF uh nee).

The word *Epiphany* means "appearance." Long ago, the birth of Christ was celebrated on the Feast of the Epiphany. Then Christ's birth date was fixed as December 25. Today, in the Eastern churches, Epiphany celebrates the baptism of Christ. In the Western churches it is a day to honor the visit of the Three Wise Men. Among many people, Epiphany is also known as Little Christmas.

Free at last!

Martin Luther King, Jr., was a famous
American civil rights leader. A Baptist
minister, he was stoned and put in jail for
practicing what he preached.

Dr. King preached that people must learn
to live together. He preached that people
should not judge others by the color of their
skin. He preached that violence is bad.

In 1964, he and his family traveled to
Norway. He was at that time the youngest
person ever to receive one of the highest of
honors—the Nobel Peace Prize.

Four years later, on April 4, 1968, Martin
Luther King was shot and killed by a hidden
rifleman. Lyndon Johnson, the President of
the United States, declared a national day of
mourning. At Dr. King's funeral, the casket
was placed on an open farm wagon. A team
of mules pulled the wagon through the streets
of Atlanta, Georgia, where Dr. King was
born in 1929.

Carved on Martin Luther King's gravestone
are words from a spiritual, similar to the
words Dr. King used in a speech he made in
Washington, D.C., in 1963. More than two
hundred thousand people had gathered at the
Lincoln Memorial to show their belief that all
people have the same rights.

Speaking to the huge crowd, Martin Luther
King said, "Free at last! Free at last! Thank
God Almighty, we are free at last!"

Hero of the South

Robert E. Lee was one of the greatest
generals of all time. He is also one of the
best-loved men in the South.

In the United States, from 1861 to 1865,
there was a long, bloody war between the
North and the South. Lee commanded an
army for the South. His men loved, trusted,
and respected him. Even though his army
was outnumbered, Lee won many battles.

Shortly before the end of the war, Lee was
made general in chief of all the Southern
armies. But it was too late. There was no way
the South could win. On April 9, 1865, Lee
was forced to give up. Seated on his famous
horse, Traveller, Lee said a sad farewell to
his soldiers.

After the war, there was still much anger
and bitterness. But Lee did his best to bring
the people of the North and South together
again. He wanted Southerners to accept being
beaten and rebuild their lives. "Make your
sons Americans," he said.

Lee spent his remaining years as president
of Washington College in Lexington, Virginia.
After he died, the college was renamed
Washington and Lee University in his honor.
Lee is buried in the college chapel. Sometimes
called "The Shrine of the South," the chapel
is visited by thousands of people each year.

On Stone Mountain, near the city of
Atlanta, Georgia, there is a huge carving of

three men on horses. One is Lee, riding his horse Traveller. The others are "Stonewall" Jackson, Lee's finest general, and Jefferson Davis, president of the Southern States. You can see pictures of the Stone Mountain Memorial in Volume 10, *Places to Know*.

Lee's birthday, January 19, is a holiday in most Southern states. But in Virginia, it is celebrated on the third Monday in January. This is because "Stonewall" Jackson, also a Virginian, was born on January 21. So Virginia celebrates the birthdays of both men on the same day—Lee-Jackson Day.

Poet of Scotland

How would you like to eat a pudding that has been cooked in a sheep's stomach? You'll certainly have a chance if you ever go to a party to celebrate the birthday of Robert Burns, the national poet of Scotland.

Every January 25, many people in Scotland and elsewhere celebrate this event in a very fitting way. Among Burns's poems is one called "To a Haggis," in which he describes this dish as that "Great chieftain o' the

puddin'-race!" So, of course, haggis must be served at the party.

Haggis tastes somewhat like hash. It is made from the heart, liver, and lungs of a sheep. These are chopped up and mixed with oatmeal, onions, and seasonings. Then everything is boiled in a bag made from the stomach of a sheep.

When the haggis is served, a man marches into the dining room playing a bagpipe. Behind him comes another man, proudly carrying the haggis on a tray. The arrival of the famous pudding is greeted with a cheer.

Australia celebrates

Clink-clank-clink. Barefoot prisoners in chains trudge along the road. All around them are guards with rifles, ready to shoot to kill.

But these people aren't really prisoners and guards. They're part of celebrations in Sydney, Australia's oldest and largest city. The marchers are showing people what it was like in Australia about two hundred years ago.

On January 26, 1788, a fleet of ships landed at what is now Sydney. These ships, under the command of Captain Arthur Phillip, had brought a load of prisoners from England.

These prisoners, or convicts as they were called, were not all desperate criminals. Some were people who had been put in jail because the government didn't like them. Some were poor people who had been arrested because they owed money. But they were the first Europeans to settle in Australia.

Since then, millions of more Europeans have chosen Australia as their homeland. And wherever they're from, they all take part in celebrating Australia Day, a national holiday, on a Monday, on or near January 26.

During the last weekend in January, Australians enjoy the folk dances and happy music of the many national groups that make up their land.

The dancers and musicians appear in the

oldest part of Sydney, called The Rocks. This hilly area is near the harbor where the first Europeans landed.

The landing in the harbor is staged every year. Nearby, the army fires cannons in honor of Australia Day.

On Australia Day, people reenact the first landing at Sydney, Australia's oldest city. The Sydney Opera House, a famous landmark, can be seen in the background.

Republic Day
January 26

India on parade

Most countries celebrate the date of their independence with one big holiday. But India celebrates with two!

One of these holidays is Independence Day. It is celebrated on August 15, the date on which India gained its independence from Great Britain in 1947 (see page 248).

Three years later, on January 26, 1950, India adopted its own constitution. This set of laws told the world that India was now an independent, democratic republic. India already had an Independence Day, so January 26 became Republic Day.

Republic Day is a national holiday. There are celebrations all over India. The biggest celebration takes place in New Delhi, the capital city. Mobs of people crowd against the ropes along the road where the parade will pass. This road is called the Raj Path, or Government Road.

The Raj Path starts at the India Gate, also known as the War Memorial Arch. The arch was built in memory of the Indian Army dead of World War I. The broad street leads

straight to government buildings that the British built when they ruled India.

The military parade may begin with a shower of rose petals from low-flying helicopters. Then marching bands begin to play and jawans (juh WAHNS), Indian soldiers, parade by in perfect order.

There are also tanks and elephants in the parade. The elephants wear clanging bells and shining beads. They carry musicians wearing brightly colored turbans. Above each elephant towers an umbrella on a long pole. The elephants are guided by trainers dressed in scarlet. These men are called mahouts (muh HOUTS).

As the parade ends, thousands of green, white, and saffron (orange-yellow) balloons— the colors of India's flag—float into the air.

For the next two days, folk dancers from all over India entertain the crowds at various places throughout New Delhi. Then the great celebration is over—until Independence Day.

The day of the Prophet

Muhammad (moo HAM uhd) was the founder of Islam, one of the world's great religions. Millions of people celebrate his birthday.

Muhammad was born in Mecca, Arabia, about the year 570. No one knows the exact date. But the date of his death is known. So the day he died is celebrated as the date of his birth.

Among many stories told of Muhammad is one about how he was named. Before he was born, his mother is said to have dreamed of many angels. The angels told her that she would have a son. She was to name the boy Muhammad, which means "Praised One."

Muhammad believed that he was the messenger of God. He thought he had been sent to call people to worship God (Allah). The religion he preached is called Islam. Islam is an Arabic word that means "submission." That is, people are to accept the will of God. People who follow the religion of Islam are called Muslims. Muslim is Arabic for "one who submits," or accepts the will of God.

In Arabic, Muhammad's birthday is called *maulid an-nabi*, which means "birthday of the Prophet." The day is one of happy festivities. Some Muslims go to a fair, where their children can enjoy the rides. Many others flock to see parades. In some countries, cannons boom and fireworks explode in the dark night sky. And Muslims everywhere feast on holiday foods.

According to the Gregorian calendar (see page 26), which is the calendar used in most parts of the world, Muhammad died on June 8, 632. On the Islamic calendar (see page 28), this is the thirteenth day of the month of Rabi I.

The Islamic calendar is based on the moon. Because of this, the time of year in which Muhammad's birthday falls keeps changing. In 1988, his birthday was celebrated in October, but by the year 2,000, it will be celebrated in June.

For Muslim children, the birthday of Muhammad is a time to enjoy the rides at a fair.

February

1

Hattie Wyatt Caraway (1878) first woman elected to the U.S. Senate

Langston Hughes (1902) American poet

2

Daniel Boone (1734) American pioneer and explorer

William Rose Benét (1886) American poet, author of "The Ballad of Jesse James"

3

Elizabeth Blackwell (1821) first woman doctor in the U.S.

Norman Rockwell (1894) American artist

4

Charles Lindbergh (1902) American aviator who was first to fly across the Atlantic alone

Rosa Lee Parks (1913) American civil rights leader

Who shares my birthday?

Is your birthday in February? The names of some of the famous people born in February are shown on the calendar on this page and the next. What do you know about the person who shares your birthday?

5

Nancy Hanks Lincoln (1784) mother of Abraham Lincoln

Henry Aaron (1934) baseball player; broke Babe Ruth's home run record

6

Ronald Reagan (1911) 40th President of the United States

Babe Ruth (1895) American baseball player and first great home run hitter

7

Laura Ingalls Wilder (1867) American author best known for her "Little House" books

8

William Sherman (1820) Union general in the Civil War

Jules Verne (1828) French author who wrote *Twenty Thousand Leagues Under the Sea*

9

William Henry Harrison (1773) 9th President of the United States

Amy Lowell (1874) American poet

10

Dame Judith Anderson (1898) Australian actress

Mark Spitz (1950) American Olympic swimmer, winner of seven gold Olympic medals

11

Thomas A. Edison (1847) American inventor

Sir Vivian Fuchs (1908) British scientist and Antarctic explorer

12

Thaddeus Kosciusko (1746) Polish patriot who fought in the American Revolution

Abraham Lincoln (1809) 16th President of the United States

13

Grant Wood (1892) American painter

Patty Berg (1918) American who became the top tournament winner in women's golf

14

Christopher Sholes (1819) American newspaperman who helped develop the typewriter

Jack Benny (1894) American entertainer

15

Galileo Galilei (1564) Italian astronomer

Susan B. Anthony (1820) American women's rights leader

16

Henry Adams (1838) American historian and writer

Edgar Bergen (1903) American ventriloquist

17

Montgomery Ward (1844) American mail-order merchant

Marian Anderson (1902) American singer

18

Mary I (1516) first queen to rule England on her own

Louis Comfort Tiffany (1848) American artist and stained-glass maker

19

Nicolaus Copernicus (1473) Polish astronomer

Carson McCullers (1917) American author of *Member of the Wedding*

20

Angelina Grimké (1805) American advocate of women's rights

Sidney Poitier (1927) first black actor to win an Academy Award

21

Barbara Jordan (1936) first black woman to serve in the Texas legislature

Alice Palmer (1855) American educator

22

George Washington (1732) 1st President of the United States

Robert Baden-Powell (1857) British soldier who founded the Boy Scouts

23

Emma Willard (1787) American educator

W. E. B. Du Bois (1866) American reformer and black historian

24

Winslow Homer (1836) American painter

Wilhelm Grimm (1786) German collector of fairy tales

25

Pierre Auguste Renoir (1841) French impressionist painter

Enrico Caruso (1873) Italian opera singer

26

Victor Hugo (1802) French author who wrote *The Hunchback of Notre Dame*

William Cody (1846) American frontiersman known as Buffalo Bill

27

Henry Wadsworth Longfellow (1807) American poet

Ralph Nader (1934) American consumer-rights advocate

28

Linus Pauling (1901) American chemist who won two Nobel Prizes

Mario Andretti (1940) Italian-born auto racer

29

Marquis de Montcalm (1712) French general; died defending Quebec

Ann Lee (1736) English religious leader of Shakers

The month to purify

February is the second and shortest month of the year. Usually, this month has only twenty-eight days. But every fourth year—called leap year—an extra day is added. This keeps the calendar in time with the seasons. If you were born on February 29, you have a real birthday only once every four years.

At one time the Roman calendar had only ten months. Then, the Romans added two months, *Januarius* (January) and *Februarius* (February). They made *Februarius* the last month of the year.

Februarius comes from the Latin word *februare*, which means "to purify," or "to make clean." It was in *Februarius* that the Romans prepared themselves for the start of the new year, which began on March 1.

Long ago, people living in England called the month *Kale-monath*. Kale is a kind of cabbage. This was the time of year when the kale plants started to appear. Later, the name was changed to *Sol-monath*, or "Sun's month," because at this time of year the sun again begins to warm the earth.

Here comes the dragon!

Firecrackers pop and crackle! Cymbals crash! Drums roll! Zigzagging down the street comes a giant golden dragon made of silk and velvet, decorated with hundreds of sparkling sequins. Twisting and turning, the dragon weaves its way through the crowds.

Chinese people are celebrating the beginning of the new year. A colorful parade—complete with floats, make-believe lions, and the golden dragon—marks the end of several days of festivities.

The Chinese New Year begins on the date of the first new moon between January 21 and February 19. This is because the ancient Chinese calendar is based on the moon (see page 29).

A large, colorful dragon is the main attraction in this Chinese New Year's parade in Washington, D.C.

People living in Chinese communities around the world observe the Chinese New Year. People in China also celebrate a three-day Spring Festival at this time.

On the Chinese New Year, a dragon and merrymakers in masks romp through the streets of Sydney, Australia.

In New York City, a masked merrymaker parades with children celebrating the Chinese New Year. The message on the banner wishes everyone a happy New Year.

Candles and weather

Candlemas Day is a special day when church candles are blessed. At one time, the people then carried lighted candles around the church. This custom goes back to the Romans, when people paraded with lighted candles at this time of year.

The Roman custom comes from a story in both Greek and Roman mythology. In the story told by the Greeks, Demeter, the goddess of farming, had a beautiful daughter named Persephone. Hades, god of the Underworld, fell in love with Persephone and carried her off. With lighted candle, Demeter roamed the world in search of her daughter.

While Persephone was with Hades, all the world turned cold and barren. Nothing would grow. Finally, Zeus, the king of the gods, arranged for Persephone to return to her mother for part of the year. Persephone's return was a sign of spring. The Greeks and Romans used this myth to explain the seasons.

People in many countries have long thought of Candlemas Day in terms of the coming of spring. An old British rhyme tells of this hope for a change in the weather:

> If Candlemas be fair and bright,
> Winter will have another flight;
> But if it is dark with clouds and rain,
> Winter is gone and will not come again.

Four-footed forecaster

Do you think that a small, furry animal can tell what the weather is going to be like? Some people in the United States think that the ground hog, or woodchuck, can.

On February 2, these people watch to see what the ground hog will do when it comes out of its snug, underground den. They think that if the ground hog is frightened by its shadow, it will crawl back into its den. If it does, there will be six more weeks of winter. But if the ground hog does not see its shadow, spring weather will come soon.

The superstition that on February 2 an animal can forecast the weather goes back hundreds of years. Long ago, farmers in Germany watched to see what badgers would

do on this date. They thought that if the badger saw its shadow and crawled back into its hole to go to sleep, there would be six more weeks of cold weather. If this happened, the farmers would be late with spring planting and have poor crops.

Naturally, everyone hoped that February 2 would be dark and cloudy so the badger would not see its shadow. Then the farmers could get ready for spring planting and look forward to a good crop.

German farmers who came to the United States brought this superstition with them. These farmers first settled in the East, where there are no badgers. But they soon discovered that the ground hog is much like the badger. So they took to watching the ground hog on February 2. And that is how the superstition about the ground hog and its shadow got started in the United States.

Is the ground hog always right? You can find out for yourself. Next February 2, note in your diary if the day is clear or cloudy. Then keep careful track of the weather during the next six weeks.

"Weeping Waters"

Hundreds of years ago, the people called Maoris (MAH oh reez) sailed their great war canoes to what is now the island country of New Zealand. According to their legends, they arrived in seven canoes known as the Great Fleet.

At first, the Maoris lived mainly by hunting and fishing. Later, they planted crops and grew some food. These people were also skilled at woodcarving. They decorated their war canoes and houses with beautiful designs.

Tall and brown-skinned, with black, wavy hair, the Maoris were proud and warlike. Each chief expected people to give in to his power. As a result, there was a great deal of fighting among the tribes.

When the first Europeans brought guns to New Zealand, the tribal wars became even

worse. But the Europeans brought more than guns. They brought disease. In less than fifty years, about half the Maoris died.

The British settlers and the Maoris wanted law and order brought to the land. So they asked Great Britain for help. Captain William Hobson of the British navy met with a group of Maori chiefs at a place named Waitangi. The name means "Weeping Waters."

On February 6, 1840, Hobson and the chiefs signed a treaty, or agreement. The Maoris agreed to accept the British queen as their ruler. In return, Great Britain would protect the lands and rights of the Maoris. Under the Treaty of Waitangi, New Zealand became a British colony.

Called Waitangi Day, February 6 marks the birth of New Zealand as a nation. It is the most important national holiday in New Zealand.

What's in a nickname?

Abraham Lincoln, the sixteenth President of the United States, had many nicknames.

As a young man, Lincoln and a friend borrowed money to buy a store. After only a few months, the store went out of business. Then Lincoln's friend died. Lincoln worked long and hard to pay back all the money himself. He finally did. This helped earn him the nickname "Honest Abe."

Another of Lincoln's nicknames was "the Railsplitter." This nickname recalled the days when, as a young man, Lincoln had split logs to make fence rails.

Lincoln became President in 1861. Soon, war began between the Northern and Southern (or Confederate) states. One reason for the war was slavery. The South had black slaves and wanted to keep them. Many people in the North wanted slavery stopped.

During the war, President Lincoln issued a law freeing all black people living under Confederate control. Because of this action, Lincoln gained the nickname "The Great Emancipator" (ih MAN suh pay tuhr), meaning "one who sets people free from slavery."

The law did not really free any slaves. Because of the war, there was no way to force people in the South to set their slaves free. But after the war was over, the law of the land was changed. A new law put an end to slavery in all parts of the nation.

Unfortunately, Lincoln did not live to see this new law passed. On the night of April 14, 1865, he was shot while at the theater. He died the next morning.

Illinois, where Lincoln lived for a long time and where he is buried, was the first state to make his birthday a holiday. Most of the states that celebrate Lincoln's birthday do so on February 12. This is the date on which he was born, in 1809, in a log cabin in Kentucky.

A few states celebrate Lincoln's birthday on the first Monday in February. Other states combine Lincoln's and Washington's birthdays. In these states, the celebration—called Presidents' Day—is held on the third Monday in February.

To my valentine

A valentine is a special way to tell someone you care. The special someone may be a sweetheart, a friend, a teacher, or your parents. Usually, a valentine has a short rhyme that tells how you feel. One valentine favorite is an old nursery rhyme:

> Roses are red, violets are blue,
> Sugar is sweet, and so are you.

A valentine also has symbols of love. These can be flowers, doves, or cupids. Cupids are chubby little children with wings. They are named for Cupid, the Roman god of love. A cupid usually has a bow and arrow. It is said that anyone struck in the heart by one of cupid's arrows will fall in love.

No one knows for certain how Valentine's Day began. Some people think that it may have come from an ancient Roman festival called Lupercalia (loo purhr KAY lee uh) celebrated on February 15. Others say that it goes back to two saints, both named Valentine. One of these saints was killed on February 14. The day was named for him.

According to one story, Valentine was thrown into jail by the Romans because he refused to worship their gods. Valentine loved children, and his young friends missed him very much. The children threw messages to him through the window of his jail cell. These messages were the first valentines.

Another lovely story links this day to the

birds. Long ago, people living in England believed that the birds picked their mates on February 14. And so the people chose this day to send messages of love to one another.

It really doesn't matter how the custom of sending valentines began. What does matter is that Valentine's Day is a wonderful chance for you to tell someone how much he or she means to you. And there's one nice thing about a valentine. You don't have to sign it if you don't want the person to know who sent it.

All of these valentines were made by children. You can make your own valentines, too. You'll see how on the next page.

Make a valentine

Materials

- construction paper
- crayons
- newspaper
- saucer
- scissors
- sponge (small)
- tempera paint

Here is a valentine you can make for someone you love. You'll find that it is easy and also fun. After you have made this valentine, try making others, using your own ideas.

1. Fold a sheet of construction paper in half. Open the paper and draw a heart. Draw it so the fold in the paper runs through the middle of the heart. Fold the paper in half, with the heart on the outside. Cut out the heart, as shown. Now you have a stencil heart and a solid heart.

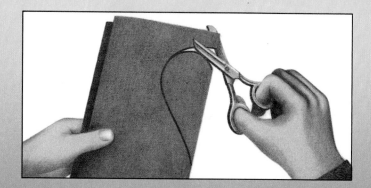

2. Cover your work table with newspaper. Stir the paint and pour a little into a saucer. Place the stencil heart over another sheet of construction paper. Dip the sponge into the paint. Hold the stencil in place with one hand while you dab the sponge lightly over the stencil heart.

3. Place the solid heart near the heart you have just printed. Use a crayon to trace around it. Write a note inside the heart you traced. Now you have a valentine for a friend or a loved one.

Eep's Valentine, Or That's What Love Is All About

by Tom McGowen

Eep the field mouse had a problem. He was desperately in love with a young lady field mouse named Squee who lived two meadows and a pond away. Squee had the longest whiskers Eep had ever seen. When she wiggled her lovely pointed nose, Eep's heart simply melted!

But the problem was that Eep was dreadfully shy. He could never seem to get up the courage to even talk to her. Whenever they met, he could only grin, foolishly, and hurry away. She probably thought he didn't even like her!

Eep's friend, Wikittiky the raccoon, tried to help. "If you could write, you could write her a letter," he suggested. "Then she'd know how you feel."

"Yes, I could do that—if I could write," Eep agreed.

"But, since you can't write," Wikittiky went on, "maybe you can find some other way to send her a message."

Eep looked hopeful. "Would you tell her for me?"

The raccoon shook his head. "That wouldn't be right. It has to come from you. That's what love is all about."

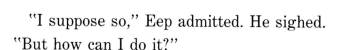

"I suppose so," Eep admitted. He sighed. "But how can I do it?"

They were both silent for a time, thinking. Then Wikittiky said, suddenly, "Send her a valentine!"

"Eh?" said Eep.

"A valentine, like the human ones give to those they like."

"Where could I get a valentine?" Eep asked.

The raccoon flicked his ear with a paw. "Make one, like the human little ones do. All you need is something red and white that looks like a heart. Easy!" Wikittiky trotted off, feeling sure he had solved Eep's problem.

But the problem wasn't quite solved. Eep
spent the next three days looking for
something red and white and heart-shaped.
He searched through his meadow. He
explored both sides of the road, and hunted in
the little patch of woods. He even gathered
enough courage to visit the outskirts of the
nearby town where the human ones lived.
Nothing. Finally, he gave up and sadly went
home.

That's when he found the apple. It was lying
in his meadow, not far from where he lived.
Probably one of the human children had
dropped it while cutting across the meadow on
the way to school. Eep went up to the apple
and looked at it. It was about four times bigger
than he was, and it was a bright and shiny red.

A bright and shiny red. And Eep knew
that it was white on the inside. Red and
white! An idea burst into his mind.

Just then, Wikittiky came ambling along.
"Nice apple," he remarked.

"Wik," said Eep, trembling with
excitement, "I have an idea. I'm going to do
it all myself, so that it'll be from me, as you
said. But I'll need your help. This apple is
much too big and heavy for me to carry, so
you'll have to carry it there for me. Will
you?"

"Sure," said Wikittiky. "But what are you
going to do?"

Eep told him. Then the little mouse went to
work.

Later that day, Squee came trotting out of

her underground home and stopped in her tracks. Right in front of her door stood a huge apple that towered over her. But it wasn't just an ordinary apple. Someone had hollowed out the inside to form a big opening the shape of a heart. The heart stood out, white against the apple's red skin.

"Why, it's a valentine!" Squee exclaimed in delight. "A valentine for me. But who could it be from?"

"It's from Eep, who lives two meadows and a pond away and is very fond of you," said Wikittiky, who was sitting nearby.

"Oh—you mean that handsome young mouse who always smiles at me but never says anything?" said Squee, more delighted than ever. "How wonderful!" She looked around. "But where is he?"

"He couldn't come," Wikittiky said, sounding a bit embarrassed. "I'm afraid he's indisposed."

Squee looked concerned. "Indisposed! Oh, dear, what's the matter with him?"

"Well—" the raccoon hesitated, then decided to tell her. "You see, Eep wanted to make this valentine for you all by himself. But to do it, he had to eat out about half the apple— which was about twice as much as he can hold! The last I saw of him he was lying flat on his back, too stuffed to move, and groaning with a bellyache!"

"Oh, dear!" Squee exclaimed. She brushed a sudden tear off her whiskers. "But—how nice to think that he would go to such trouble and discomfort for me!"

"Well," said Wikittiky, wisely, "that's what love is all about!"

The right to vote

Down through the years, pictures of famous men—mostly presidents—have appeared on American money. Finally, from 1979-1981, the U.S. government minted a coin with the picture of a woman on it. The coin was a dollar, and the woman was Susan B. Anthony. She is famous because she fought to give women the same rights as men.

Susan B. Anthony was born on February 15, 1820. At that time, women had few rights under the law. In most states, women could not own property or vote. When Susan Anthony grew up, she worked for equal rights for women—especially the right to vote.

Susan B. Anthony voted in the 1872 election for President. A few weeks later, she was arrested. At that time, women were not allowed to vote.

This U.S. coin is the Susan B. Anthony dollar.

Susan Anthony did not live to see her dream come true. She died in 1906, fourteen years before women won the right to vote. She is so admired for her work that some states and many schools celebrate Susan B. Anthony Day on February 15, her birthday.

Other states honor her on August 26, Women's Equality Day, the date on which the 19th Amendment was made part of the U.S. Constitution. This law gave all women in the United States the right to vote.

"Let's go to the Rondy!"

Rondy is short for *rendezvous*—a place where people get together. It's the Anchorage Fur Rendezvous, the most popular celebration in Alaska.

The Rondy began as a three-day sports carnival. Trappers brought their furs into town by dog sled. They sold the furs and held sled-dog races.

Now, the Rondy is a ten-day winter carnival that Alaskans enjoy in February. There is something for everyone. Each day is like a holiday. You see Indians dance and Eskimos bounce sky-high as they're tossed on a blanket made of walrus skins.

You see parades, night and day. You see men in fur hats and fur-lined parkas. They grow bushy beards to see who'll become "Mr. Fur Face."

Furs aren't as important as they used to be at the Rondy. Still, there are outdoor fur

Meet "Mr. Fur Face"! The title is awarded each year in a beard-growing contest at the Rondy.

auctions, a fur-hat contest, and a fur style show. Other events range from an ice show to stock car races on ice.

Then what's the most important event at the Rondy? It's sled-dog races! There are sled-dog races for older children and a Women's World Championship Race. But the main event is the World's Championship Sled Dog Races that run for the last three days of the Rondy.

The changing birthday

It's a good old American custom to enjoy cherry pie on Washington's birthday. But do you know why?

The custom probably began because of a story told about America's first President. According to this tale, young George chopped down one of his father's cherry trees. When his father asked who had done it, George confessed. He is supposed to have said, "Father, I cannot tell a lie."

Like many stories about Washington, this one probably isn't true. But people loved and admired Washington. They were willing to believe almost anything about his honesty and goodness.

Today, Washington's birthday is on February 22. But this is not the date on which he was born. When Washington was born, people in England and America did not use the calendar used today (see page 24). According to the calendar then in use, Washington was born on February 11, 1731.

In 1752, England and America switched to the calendar used today. This meant dropping eleven days. So, what would have been September 3, 1752, became September 14. At the same time, New Year's Day was changed from March 25 to January 1.

People born before 1752 were to add eleven days to the date of their birth. And if they were born between January 1 and March 25 they were to add one year. So, Washington's birthday became February 22, 1732 instead of February 11, 1731.

As you might expect, most people were slow to change their birthday. For many years, Washington continued to celebrate his birthday on February 11. But by the time he became President, he and others celebrated his birthday on February 22.

Things stayed this way for many years. But since 1971, this holiday has been celebrated on the third Monday in February. This change was made so that people could enjoy a three-day weekend.

George Washington led the American Army to victory over the British in the Revolutionary War.

At the Mardi Gras in New Orleans, people grab for trinkets that are tossed from the parade floats.

Carnival time!

The world's turned topsy-turvy! It's snowing bits of paper. Clowns are dancing with witches. And kings and queens walk hand-in-hand with beggars. It's the Mardi Gras (MAHR dee grah) carnival. Everyone roams the streets wearing a costume and mask. And everyone parades and goes to parties.

Mardi Gras is French for "Fat Tuesday." The name comes from the old custom of parading a fat ox through the streets of Paris on this day. The ox was to remind the people that they were not to eat meat during Lent—the time from Ash Wednesday (see page 96) to Easter Sunday (see page 142).

Mardi Gras can be as early as February 3 or as late as March 9. The exact date depends on the date set for Easter Sunday.

French people who came to America brought with them the custom of celebrating Mardi Gras. The most famous Mardi Gras carnival in the United States is at New Orleans, Louisiana. There are also carnivals and parades in Biloxi, Mississippi, Mobile, Alabama, and other cities.

Merrymakers in France still enjoy the fun of Mardi Gras. So do people in places as far apart as Viareggio in Italy and Rio de Janeiro in Brazil.

There is also a famous Mardi Gras carnival in the little town of Binche in Belgium. There,

In southern Italy, the people dress up in costumes and put on an ancient play during Mardi Gras.

the people dress in colorful clown costumes. On their heads they wear tall bunches of ostrich feathers. As the clowns, or *gilles* as they are called, dance down the street, the bells hanging from their belts jingle and jangle. The *gilles* also carry baskets of oranges. As they dance along, they throw oranges to the watching crowd.

Mardi Gras is also known as Shrove Tuesday. This name comes from the custom of confessing one's sins on the day before Lent begins. *Shrove* means "forgiven one's sins."

During Mardi Gras, people in Rio de Janeiro, Brazil, dance in the streets.

People in Nice, France, wear giant masks in the Mardi Gras parade.

Pancake Day

They're off!

Many people in the United Kingdom eat pancakes on Shrove Tuesday, the day before Ash Wednesday, when Lent begins. The custom began long ago, when people could not eat butter and eggs during Lent. So, to use up their butter and eggs before Ash Wednesday (see page 96), they made pancakes.

On Pancake Day, as it is called, the women of Olney, England, have a pancake race. On this day, the women line up in the market

square. Each carries a pancake in a frying pan. The women must flip their pancakes three times as they race for the church door at the other end of the square.

A bell clangs. They're off! Pancakes are flipping and feet are flying. The race lasts about a minute. The winner gets a kiss from the bell ringer of the village.

On the same day, there is also a pancake race in Liberal, Kansas. The people of Olney and the people of Liberal compare winning times by telephone to see which town has won the pancake race.

The beginning of Lent

Ash Wednesday is the first day of Lent. It can be as early as February 4 or as late as March 10. The exact date depends on the date set for Easter Sunday (see page 142).

Ash Wednesday is observed in Roman Catholic churches and in some Protestant churches. In Roman Catholic churches, ashes from burned palm leaves are blessed. A priest then uses these ashes to mark a cross on each person's forehead. The ashes are to remind people that they came from dust and will one day return to dust.

Lent is a religious season that is a time of fasting (not eating as much food as usual) and of prayer. Lent begins on Ash Wednesday, forty days before Easter (not counting Sundays) and ends on Easter Sunday. The forty days of Lent are to remind people of the forty days Jesus fasted in the wilderness. The word Lent comes from the Old English word *lencten*, which means "spring."

In many countries, special foods are eaten during Lent. These foods are usually a substitute for meat. In Ireland, people have a dish called champ. It is made up of scallions, a kind of onion, whipped in with hot mashed potatoes and served with a lump of butter in the middle.

The English also make special foods for

The ashes used in Ash Wednesday services come from burned palm leaves.

Lent. One is a pudding of flour and milk, flavored with fruit syrups. Because it can be made quickly, it is known as hasty pudding.

In most places, fish is a standard food throughout Lent. So are eggs. But there was a time when people were forbidden to eat fish, eggs, and butter, as well as meat. During the forty weekdays of Lent they could have only bread and water.

Many religious groups have times of fasting. Jews fast on Yom Kippur, the Day of Atonement (see page 264). Muslims fast during the month of Ramadan (see page 208).

March

1

Blanche Kelso Bruce (1841) first full-term black American senator

Harry Belafonte (1927) American singer famous for West Indian songs

2

Dr. Seuss (1904) American author and illustrator (real name Theodor Seuss Geisel) who wrote *The Cat in the Hat* and other books

3

Alexander Graham Bell (1847) American inventor of the telephone

4

Casimir Pulaski (1747) Polish patriot; hero of the American Revolution

Knute Rockne (1888) American football coach at Notre Dame

Who shares my birthday?

Is your birthday in March? The names of some of the famous people born in March are shown on the calendar on this page and the next. What do you know about the person who shares your birthday?

5

Howard Pyle (1853) American writer and illustrator of *The Merry Adventures of Robin Hood* and other children's books

6

Elizabeth Barrett Browning (1806) English poet

Valentina Tereshkova (1937) Soviet cosmonaut; first woman to travel in space

7

Tomáš Masaryk (1850) Czech statesman

Janet Guthrie (1938) American auto racer; first woman to race in the Indianapolis 500

8

Oliver Wendell Holmes, Jr. (1841) American judge who served on the U.S. Supreme Court for nearly thirty years

9

Amerigo Vespucci (1454) Italian explorer for whom America was named

10

William Etty (1787) English painter

Arthur Honegger (1892) French composer

11

Wanda Gág (1893) American author and illustrator who wrote *Millions of Cats*

Ralph Abernathy (1926) American civil rights leader and clergyman

12

Jane Delano (1862) American nurse; organized Red Cross Nursing Service

Walter Schirra, Jr. (1923) American astronaut

13

Joseph Priestley (1733) English chemist

Johann Wyss (1781) Swiss who finished his father's book *The Swiss Family Robinson*

14

Albert Einstein (1879) German-born scientist

Marguerite de Angeli (1889) American author and illustrator

15

Andrew Jackson (1767) 7th President of the United States

Harry James (1916) American trumpeter

16

James Madison
(1751) 4th President
of the United States

Jerry Lewis (1926)
American comedian

17

Jim Bridger (1804)
American frontier
scout

Kate Greenaway
(1846) English
illustrator of
children's books

18

Grover Cleveland
(1837) 22nd and 24th
President of the
United States

Rudolf Diesel
(1858) German
inventor of the diesel
engine

19

David Livingstone
(1813) British
missionary who
explored Africa

**William Jennings
Bryan** (1860)
American political
leader

20

Henrik Ibsen
(1828) Norwegian
playwright

Lauritz Melchior
(1890) Danish tenor

21

Benito Juárez
(1806) Mexican
political leader and
president

Phyllis McGinley
(1905) American
poet, best known for
her light verse

22

**Randolph
Caldecott** (1846)
English illustrator of
children's books

Marcel Marceau
(1923) French mime

23

Fannie Farmer
(1857) American
cooking expert

**Sir Roger
Bannister** (1929)
British athlete; ran a
mile in less than four
minutes

24

**John Wesley
Powell** (1834)
American explorer of
the Grand Canyon

Harry Houdini
(1874) American
magician and escape
artist

25

Arturo Toscanini
(1867) Italian
symphony conductor

Gloria Steinem
(1934) American
writer; founder of
Ms. magazine

26

Robert Frost (1874)
American poet

**Sandra Day
O'Connor** (1930)
American jurist; first
woman U.S.
Supreme Court
justice

27

Nathaniel Currier
(1813) American
printmaker who
pictured life in the
U.S. in the 1800's

Wilhelm Roentgen
(1845) German who
discovered X rays

28

Raphael (1483)
Italian artist and
chief architect of St.
Peter's cathedral in
Rome

George I (1660)
king of England

29

John Tyler (1790)
10th President of the
United States

Pearl Bailey (1918)
American singer

30

Francisco Goya
(1746) Spanish
painter

Jo Davidson (1883)
American sculptor

31

Joseph Haydn
(1732) Austrian
composer

Jack Johnson
(1878) American
boxer, the first black
heavyweight champion

The month of Mars

March, the third month of the year, has thirty-one days.

On the Roman calendar, the year began with March. Romans named the month after Mars, their god of war, because springtime was when they prepared to go off to war.

Until a little more than two hundred years ago, March 25 was New Year's Day in England and America. Then the new calendar was adopted and January became the first month of the year.

In England, long ago, people called March *Lencten-monath*, meaning "Lengthening month." After the first day of spring (March 20 or 21), the days do grow longer.

In the northern half of the world, people often say that "March comes in like a lion and goes out like a lamb." This means that the weather in early March is often stormy, but by the end, it is mild. In the southern part of the world, March marks the beginning of fall.

The mark of a Welshman

The fierce battle had raged for hours. Swords clashed as the men of Wales fought to protect their land from the Saxon invaders. But the Welsh were losing.

A monk with the Welsh army thought he knew why. Both sides wore the same kind of clothing. It was hard to tell a friend from an enemy.

But the monk had an idea. As the Welsh warriors began to retreat, he called them together. "Welshmen," he cried, "you must mark yourselves so that you can quickly tell who is a Welshman and who is a Saxon."

The monk reached down and pulled a leek plant from the ground. "Let each man wear a leek. Then you will know that any man who is not wearing a leek is an enemy!"

Soon, all the Welsh soldiers were wearing leeks. Again they charged the enemy. Before long, the Welsh won the battle. They had kept their country free.

The monk who saved the day was named David. After his death, the Catholic Church made him a saint. He became the patron saint of Wales. And the day of his death, March 1, became St. David's Day.

No one knows if the story of David and the leek is true. But the leek is the national flower of Wales. And in Wales, St. David's Day is a holiday. On that day, Welsh people all over the world proudly wear the stalk, a flower, or a bit of leaf from a leek plant.

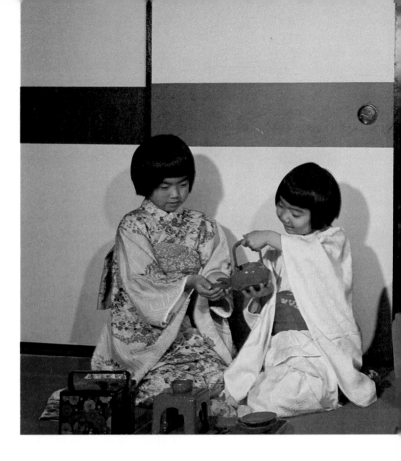

A day for
girls and dolls

Japan is a land of many beautiful festivals.
The Japanese word for festival is *matsuri*. A
favorite festival for girls is *Hina Matsuri*,
held on March 3. *Hina* is the Japanese name
for a special set of dolls that families with
girls put on display on *Hina Matsuri*, or
Dolls' Festival. These dolls are not to play
with. They are very valuable, and are often
handed down from mother to daughter.

The dolls are always arranged in a special
way. Usually, the mother does this for her
daughter or daughters. A series of shelves,

On Dolls' Festival, families with girls display a special set of dolls that stand for the royal court of Japan.

The two most important dolls in the set stand for the emperor and the empress of Japan.

looking much like steps, is set up. The stand is then covered with red cloth.

On the top shelf, in the place of honor, are the emperor and the empress. Below them are members of the royal court. First, there are three ladies in waiting. Then there are five musicians, two officials, and, finally, three guardsmen.

Placed among the dolls are tiny pieces of furniture, musical instruments, and decorated boxes. There are also fresh peach blossoms and food offerings, such as cakes and candy in the shape of fruits. In the set shown here, there is even a tiny, horse-drawn carriage.

After the festival, everything is carefully packed away until the next year.

*This young girl is getting clown makeup put on
during the Moomba Festival in Melbourne, Australia.*

Moomba!

Moomba means "get together and have fun."
And that's just what the people of Melbourne,
Australia, do at the yearly Moomba Festival.

The Moomba Festival gets its name from
the language of the Aborigines, who were the
first people to live in Australia. The festival
runs for eleven days. And there is something
for everyone.

Among the many events are water shows
and boat races on the Yarra river, which

Australian children often take part in the Moomba parade. These youngsters are riding unicycles.

flows through the city. At Melbourne Cricket Ground, children's teams play many different sports. There are games of cricket, which is a favorite sport in Australia, as well as soccer, rugby and football. And children's plays are put on at an outdoor theatre.

The busy festival ends with a big parade on Labor Day, the second Monday in March. Bagpipe bands play lively marches and there are gaily decorated floats. The Moomba King and Queen lead the parade. And everywhere there are clowns and more clowns.

The people of Melbourne really know what *moomba* means!

The wearing of the green

On St. Patrick's Day, you may hear such Irish songs as "The Wearing of the Green." And on this day, many people—even some who are not Irish—do wear something green.

The bit of green is a reminder of the

Irish wolfhounds, the tallest of all dogs, lead the St. Patrick's Day parade in New York City.

beautiful green countryside of Ireland. This island nation is so green that it is often called the Emerald Isle. (An emerald is a lovely green jewel.) Green is also the color of the shamrock, a small cloverlike plant with three leaves on each stem. It is the national symbol of Ireland.

In Ireland, St. Patrick's Day is both a holy day and holiday. Saint Patrick, Ireland's patron saint, brought Christianity to Ireland. According to legend, he used the three leaves of the shamrock to explain the idea of the Trinity—that in the one God there are three divine Persons: the Father, the Son, and the Holy Spirit. Another legend says that Saint Patrick rid Ireland of snakes by charming them into the sea.

St. Patrick's Day is usually celebrated with a parade. The one in Dublin, Ireland, has come to be known as the Irish Mardi Gras. The St. Patrick's Day Parade in New York City is perhaps the biggest.

Two big Irish wolfhounds always lead the marchers in the gala New York City parade. These huge dogs are the mascots of the Fighting 69th, an infantry regiment that is part of the New York National Guard. At one time, this regiment was made up entirely of Irishmen. More than a hundred bands and a hundred thousand marchers follow the dogs up Fifth Avenue. The parade lasts for hours.

You don't have to be Irish to celebrate St. Patrick's Day. Next March 17, put on a shamrock or a bit of green and have fun.

The Peddler of Ballaghaderreen

by Ruth Sawyer

Ruth Sawyer, author and storyteller, collected many folktales in Ireland. Here is a story she heard from John Hegarty, who was a Donegal shanachie, or travelling storyteller. Ballaghaderreen, which means "the road of the little oak wood," is a town in County Roscommon, Ireland.

More years ago than you can tell me and twice as many as I can tell you, there lived a peddler in Ballaghaderreen. He lived at the crossroads, by himself in a bit of a cabin with one room to it, and that so small that a man could stand in the middle of the floor and, without taking a step, he could lift the latch on the front door, he could lift the latch on the back door, and he could hang the kettle over the turf. That is how small and snug it was.

Outside the cabin the peddler had a bit of a garden. In it he planted carrots and cabbages,

onions and potatoes. In the center grew a
cherry tree—as brave and fine a tree as you
would find anywhere in Ireland. Every spring
it flowered, the white blossoms covering it
like a fresh falling of snow. Every summer it
bore cherries as red as heart's blood.

But every year, after the garden was
planted the wee brown hares would come
from the copse nearby and nibble-nibble here,
and nibble-nibble there, until there was not a
thing left, barely, to grow into a full-sized
vegetable that a man could harvest for his
table. And every summer as the cherries
began to ripen the blackbirds came in
whirling flocks and ate the cherries as fast as
they ripened.

The neighbors that lived thereabouts
minded this and nodded their heads and said:

"Master Peddler, you're a poor, simple man, entirely. You let the wild creatures thieve from you without lifting your hand to stop them."

And the peddler would always nod his head back at them and laugh and answer: "Nay, then, 'tis not thieving they are at all. They pay well for what they take. Look you—on yonder cherry tree the blackbirds sing sweeter nor they sing on any cherry tree in Ballaghaderreen. And the brown hares make good company at dusk-hour for a lonely man."

In the country roundabout, every day when there was market, a wedding, or a fair, the peddler would be off at ring-o'-day, his pack strapped on his back, one foot ahead of the other, fetching him along the road. And when he reached the town diamond he would open his pack, spread it on the green turf, and, making a hollow of his two hands, he would call:

"Come buy a trinket—come buy a
        brooch—
Come buy a kerchief of scarlet or
        yellow!"

In no time at all there would be a great crowding of lads and lasses and children about him, searching his pack for what they might be wanting. And like as not, some barefooted lad would hold up a jackknife and ask: "How much for this, Master Peddler?"

And the peddler would answer: "Half a crown."

And the lad would put it back, shaking his

head dolefully. "Faith, I haven't the half of that, nor likely ever to have it."

And the peddler would pull the lad over to him and whisper in his ear: "Take the knife—'twill rest a deal more easy in your pocket than in my pack."

Then, like as not, some lass would hold up a blue kerchief to her yellow curls and ask: "Master Peddler, what is the price of this?"

And the peddler would answer: "One shilling sixpence."

And the lass would put it back, the smile gone from her face, and she turning away.

And the peddler would catch up the kerchief again and tie it himself about her curls and laugh and say: "Faith, there it looks far prettier than ever it looks in my pack. Take it, with God's blessing."

So it would go—a brooch to this one and a top to that. There were days when the peddler

took in little more than a few farthings. But after those days he would sing his way homeward; and the shrewd ones would watch him passing by and wag their fingers at him and say: "You're a poor, simple man, Master Peddler. You'll never be putting a penny by for your old age. You'll end your days like the blackbirds, whistling for crumbs at our back doors. Why, even the vagabond dogs know they can wheedle the half of the bread you are carrying in your pouch, you're that simple."

Which likewise was true. Every stray, hungry dog knew him the length and breadth of the county. Rarely did he follow a road without one tagging his heels, sure of a noonday sharing of bread and cheese.

There were days when he went abroad without his pack, when there was no market day, no wedding or fair. These he spent with the children, who would have followed him about like the dogs, had their mothers let them. On these days he would sit himself down on some doorstep and when a crowd of children had gathered he would tell them tales—old tales of Ireland—tales of the good folk, of the heroes, of the saints. He knew them all, and he knew how to tell them, the way the children would never be forgetting one of them, but carry them in their hearts until they were old.

And whenever he finished a tale he would say, like as not, laughing and pinching the cheek of some wee lass: "Mind well your manners, whether you are at home or abroad, for you can never be telling what good folk, or saint, or hero you may be fetching up with on the road—or who may come knocking at your doors. Aye, when Duirmuid, or Fionn or Oisin or Saint Patrick walked the earth they were poor and simple and plain men; it took death to put a grand memory on them. And the poor and the simple and the old today may be heroes tomorrow—you never can be telling. So keep a kind word for all, and a gentling hand."

Often an older would stop to listen to the scraps of words he was saying; and often as not he would go his way, wagging his finger and mumbling: "The poor, simple man. He's as foolish as the blackbirds."

Spring followed winter in Ireland, and summer followed close upon the heels of both. And winter came again and the peddler grew old. His pack grew lighter and lighter, until the neighbors could hear the trinkets jangling inside as he passed, so few things were left. They would nod their heads and say to one another: "Like as not his pockets are as empty as his pack. Time will come, with winter at hand, when he will be at our back doors begging crumbs, along with the blackbirds."

The time did come, as the neighbors had prophesied it would, smug and proper, when the peddler's pack was empty, when he had naught in his pockets and naught in his cupboard. That night he went hungry to bed.

Now it is more than likely that hungry men will dream; and the peddler of Ballaghaderreen had a strange dream that night. He dreamed that there came a sound of knocking in the middle of the night. Then the latch on the front door lifted, the door opened without a creak or a cringe, and inside the cabin stepped Saint Patrick. Standing in the doorway the good man pointed a finger; and he spoke in a voice tuned as low as the wind over the bogs. "Peddler, peddler of Ballaghaderreen, take the road to Dublin Town. When you get to the bridge that spans the Liffey you will hear what you were meant to hear."

On the morrow the peddler awoke and remembered the dream. He rubbed his stomach and found it mortal empty; he stood on his legs and found them trembling in under him; and he said to himself: "Faith, an empty stomach and weak legs are the worst traveling companions a man can have, and Dublin is a long way. I'll bide where I am."

That night the peddler went hungrier to bed, and again came the dream. There came the

knocking on the door, the lifting of the latch.
The door opened and Saint Patrick stood there,
pointing the road: "Peddler, peddler of
Ballaghaderreen, take the road that leads to
Dublin Town. When you get to the bridge that
spans the Liffey you will hear what you were
meant to hear!"

The second day it was the same as the first.
The peddler felt the hunger and the weakness
stronger in him, and stayed where he was. But

when he woke after the third night and the third coming of the dream, he rose and strapped his pack from long habit upon his back and took the road to Dublin. For three long weary days he traveled, barely staying his fast, and on the fourth day he came into the city.

Early in the day he found the bridge spanning the river and all the lee-long day he stood there, changing his weight from one foot to the other, shifting his pack to ease the drag of it, scanning the faces of all who passed by. But although a great tide of people swept this way, and a great tide swept that, no one stopped and spoke to him.

At the end of the day he said to himself: "I'll find me a blind alley, and like an old dog I'll lay me down in it and die." Slowly he moved off the bridge. As he passed by the Head Inn of Dublin, the door opened and out came the landlord.

To the peddler's astonishment he crossed the thoroughfare and hurried after him. He clapped a strong hand on his shoulder and cried: "Arra, man hold a minute! All day I've been watching you. All day I have seen you standing on the bridge like an old rook with rent wings. And of all the people passing from the west to the east, and of all the people passing from the east to the west, not one crossing the bridge spoke aught with you. Now I am filled with a great curiosity entirely to know what fetched you here."

Seeing hunger and weariness on the peddler, he drew him toward the inn. "Come; in return for having my curiosity satisfied you shall have rest in the kitchen yonder, with bread and cheese and ale. Come."

So the peddler rested his bones by the kitchen hearth and he ate as he hadn't eaten in many days. He was satisfied at long last and the landlord repeated his question. "Peddler, what fetched you here?"

"For three nights running I had a dream—" began the peddler, but he got no further.

The landlord of the Head Inn threw back his head and laughed. How he laughed, rocking on his feet, shaking the whole length of him!

"A dream you had, by my soul, a dream!" He spoke when he could get his breath. "I could be telling you were the cut of a man to have dreams, and to listen to them, what's more. Rags on your back and hunger in your cheeks and age upon you, and I'll wager not a farthing in your pouch. Well, God's blessing on you and your dreams."

The peddler got to his feet, saddled his pack, and made for the door. He had one foot over the sill when the landlord hurried after him and again clapped a hand on his shoulder.

"Hold, Master Peddler," he said, "I too had a dream, three nights running." He burst into laughter again, remembering it. "I dreamed there came a knocking on this very door, and the latch lifted, and, standing in the doorway, as you are standing, I saw Saint Patrick. He pointed with one finger to the road running westward and he said: 'Landlord, Landlord of the Head Inn, take *that* road to Ballaghaderreen. When you come to the crossroads you will find a wee cabin, and beside the cabin a wee garden, and in the center of the garden a cherry tree. Dig deep under the tree and you will find gold—much gold.'"

The landlord paused and drew his sleeve across his mouth to hush his laughter.

"Ballaghaderreen! I never heard of the place. Gold under a cherry tree—whoever heard of gold under a cherry tree! There is only one dream that I hear, waking or sleeping, and it's the dream of gold, much gold, in my own pocket. Aye, listen, 'tis a good dream." And the landlord thrust a hand into his pouch and jangled the coins loudly in the peddler's ear.

Back to Ballaghaderreen went the peddler,
one foot ahead of the other. How he got there I
cannot be telling you. He unslung his pack, took
up a mattock lying nearby, and dug under the
cherry tree. He dug deep and felt at last the
scraping of the mattock against something hard
and smooth. It took him time to uncover it and
he found it to be an old sea chest, of foreign
pattern and workmanship, bound around with
bands of brass. These he broke, and lifting the
lid he found the chest full of gold, tarnished

and clotted with mold; pieces of six and pieces
of eight and Spanish doubloons.

I cannot begin to tell the half of the goodness
that the peddler put into the spending of that
gold. But this I know. He built a chapel at the
crossroads—a resting place for all weary
travelers journeying thither.

And after he had gone the neighbors had a
statue made of him and placed it facing the
crossroads. And there he stands to this day, a
pack on his back and a dog at his heels.

Welcome to our table!

March 19 is a holiday in Italy. It's a day that honors Saint Joseph. He was the carpenter from Nazareth who was chosen to be the husband of the Virgin Mary.

In villages throughout Italy, and especially on the island of Sicily, it is the custom to set up a "Saint Joseph's Table." Townspeople load a large table with food. Spaghetti, lasagne, and ravioli are served, along with special desserts, fruits, and wine.

Three people are picked to play the parts of Jesus, Mary, and Joseph. They welcome everyone to the table. Guests of honor include orphans, widows, and beggars.

Italians in other parts of the world also follow the custom of setting up a "Saint Joseph's Table." And many Italians wear something red on St. Joseph's Day, just as the Irish wear something green on St. Patrick's Day.

St. Joseph's Day is also a holiday in Spain. In the Spanish city of Valencia, this holiday ends a week of festivity. During the week, there are fireworks, parades, and street dances. The streets and squares are decorated with huge figures of animals and people made of cardboard, wood, or papier-mâché. Around midnight on St. Joseph's Day, the city lights up with a fiery blaze as all these figures are burned.

During St. Joseph's falla, or celebration, the streets of Valencia, Spain are decorated with huge statues.

When he was president of Mexico, Benito Juárez traveled about in a black horsedrawn carriage.

**Birthday of
Benito Juárez**
March 21

The man in the black carriage

Benito Juárez (behn EE toh HWAH rehs) was one of the greatest leaders in the history of Mexico. His birthday, on March 21, is celebrated as a national holiday.

Juárez was born in a small village in the year 1806. His parents, who were Zapotec (ZAH puh tehk) Indians, were very poor. They died when Juárez was only three years old.

As a young boy, Juárez worked in the fields with an uncle. Juárez could not read or write. He spoke only his Indian language.

When Juárez was twelve, he went to the city of Oaxaca in southern Mexico. There he found a job and began to go to school. In time, he became a lawyer and went into politics. In 1861, he was elected president.

The following year, the French invaded Mexico. When they captured Mexico City, Juárez fled for his life. Traveling about in his black carriage, he continued to lead the fight for his country's freedom.

The French made an Austrian duke, Maximilian (mack suh MIHL ih uhn), the emperor of Mexico. He gave orders to shoot all followers of Juárez on sight.

Finally, in 1866, the United States forced the French to leave Mexico. Mexican troops captured Maximilian and he was shot by a firing squad. Juárez, still traveling in his plain black carriage, returned to Mexico City and his office in the National Palace. Today, the president still has an office there. But now, part of the Palace is the Juárez museum.

There is a statue of Juárez in Washington, D.C. It was a gift from the people of Mexico to the people of the United States. On the base of the statue are these words by Juárez: "Respect for the rights of others is peace."

Liberty—or death!

Today, Greece is a free country. But for hundreds of years, the Greeks suffered under the rule of Turkey.

Then, on March 25, 1821, a group of Greek leaders met in a church. They took a vow—liberty or death! At the same time, another group issued a declaration of independence. Finally, in 1829, after eight long years of war, the Greeks won their freedom from Turkey and became an independent nation.

In Athens, the capital of Greece, there is a big military parade on March 25 to celebrate Independence Day. Among the marchers are the world-famous evzones (EHV zohns).

The evzones are special and very colorful Greek soldiers. Evzones wear a red cap with a black tassel, a colored vest over a white shirt, a white pleated skirt over white tights, and red shoes with a black pompon at the toe.

All about, whipping in the breeze, are Greek flags. The Greek flag has a white cross on a sky-blue field. The cross stands for the Greek Orthodox Church—the religion followed by most of the people in Greece. In Greece, the church and the state are very close. This is especially true on March 25.

In the religious calendar, March 25 is the Feast of the Annunciation. Annunciation (uh nuhn see AY shun) means "to tell" or "to make an announcement." According to Christian belief, this is the date on which the Angel

Pleat-skirted evzones are a major attraction in the Independence Day parade in Athens. Originally chosen as a royal guard, this unit of the Greek Army performs many special tasks, such as standing guard at the Tomb of the Unknown Soldier.

Gabriel told the Virgin Mary that she was to be the mother of Jesus Christ.

So, in Greece, March 25 is doubly important. It is both a national holiday and a religious feast day.

Haman's hat

Would you like to wear a mask and a costume on a holiday that's not Halloween? Jewish children do this on a holiday called Purim (POO rihm), or the Feast of Lots.

This merry holiday falls on the fourteenth day of the Hebrew month of Adar, which comes in February or March. Jewish people everywhere celebrate Purim with great joy. It is a happy time, for it recalls how good Queen Esther saved the Jews from death.

The full story is in the Book of Esther in the Bible. This story is read on Purim, at home and in places of worship called synagogues (SIHN uh gawgs).

Long ago, in Persia (now Iran), there was a wicked man named Haman. Haman was angered when Queen Esther's cousin, a Jew, refused to bow before him. To get even,

At Purim, children enjoy three-cornered pastries called Hamantashen. *These pastries are filled with fruit and nuts, or with poppy seeds and honey.*

Haman plotted to kill all Jews. The day was to be decided by lot. (A lot is a piece of paper that is picked by chance in order to decide something.) But Queen Esther pleaded with her husband, the king, and saved her people.

When the story of Esther is read on Purim, people often follow an ancient custom. Everytime Haman's name is mentioned, they stamp their feet or rattle a noisemaker to show how they feel about him.

The joy of Purim is shown in other ways, too. Gifts are given to friends and the needy. And children put on plays that tell the story of Queen Esther.

In the evening, family and friends sit down for a happy Purim feast. Among the foods enjoyed are three-cornered pastries called *Hamentashen,* or "Haman's hat"—even though *hamantashen* really means "Haman's pockets." And sometimes these goodies are even called "Haman's ears"!

April

2

3

5

8

10

1

William Harvey
(1578) English
doctor; discovered
blood circulation

**Sergei
Rachmaninoff**
(1873) Russian
composer

2

**Hans Christian
Andersen** (1805)
Danish writer of
fairy tales

Frédéric Bartholdi
(1834) French sculptor
who designed the
Statue of Liberty

3

Washington Irving
(1783) American
author who wrote
"Rip Van Winkle"

Jane Goodall (1934)
British ethologist
noted for her study of
chimpanzees

4

Dorothea Dix
(1802) American who
worked to help the
mentally ill and to
improve prisons

Linus Yale, Jr.
(1821) American
inventor of locks

Who shares
my birthday?

Is your birthday in April? The names of
some of the famous people born in April
are shown on the calendar on this page and
the next. What do you know about the
person who shares your birthday?

5

**Booker T.
Washington** (1856)
American black
leader and educator

W. Atlee Burpee
(1858) started first
mail-order seed
company in Canada

6

Lowell Thomas
(1892) American
radio and TV reporter

**James Dewey
Watson** (1928)
American biologist;
one of the builders of
DNA model

7

**William
Wordsworth** (1770)
English poet

Gabriela Mistral
(1889) Chilean poet
(real name Lucila
Alcayaga)

8

Mary Pickford
(1893) Canadian-born
actress known as
"America's
Sweetheart"

Sonja Henie (1912)
Norwegian champion
Olympic figure skater

9

Charles Steinmetz
(1865) German-born
electrical engineer

Paul Robeson
(1898) American
actor and singer

10

William Booth
(1829) English
founder of the
Salvation Army

Clare Boothe Luce
(1903) American
writer and diplomat

11

Percy Julian (1899)
American research
chemist

Stella Walsh (1911)
Polish-born athlete
who set many world
records

12

Henry Clay (1777)
American statesman

Frederic Melcher
(1879) American
publisher; founder of
Children's Book
Week

13

Thomas Jefferson
(1743) 3rd President
of the United States

Marguerite Henry
(1902) American
author of children's
books

14

Christian Huygens
(1629) Dutch physicist

Anne Sullivan
(1866) American
teacher of Helen
Keller; writer and
champion of the blind

15

Leonardo da Vinci
(1452) Italian painter,
sculptor, and
scientist

**Harold
Washington** (1922)
first black mayor of
Chicago

16

Wilbur Wright (1867) American who, with brother Orville, invented the airplane

Kareem Abdul-Jabbar (1947) American basketball star

17

J. P. Morgan (1837) American banker

Nikita Khrushchev (1894) Soviet premier

18

Clarence S. Darrow (1857) American criminal lawyer

Leopold Stokowski (1882) English-born orchestra conductor

19

Roger Sherman (1721) only person to sign four documents of American independence

Jean Lee Latham (1902) American author

20

Daniel C. French (1850) American sculptor of *The Minute Man*

Joan Miró (1893) Spanish painter

21

Friedrich Froebel (1782) German founder of kindergarten system

Elizabeth II (1926) queen of Great Britain

22

Isabella I (1451) Spanish queen who helped Columbus

J. Robert Oppenheimer (1904) American developer of the atomic bomb

23

James Buchanan (1791) 15th President of the United States

Lester B. Pearson (1897) a Canadian prime minister

24

Barbra Streisand (1942) American singer and actress

25

Guglielmo Marconi (1874) Italian who developed wireless telegraphy

Ella Fitzgerald (1918) American jazz singer

26

John James Audubon (1785) American naturalist and painter

Carol Burnett (1934) American entertainer

27

Ulysses S. Grant (1822) 18th President of the United States

Coretta Scott King (1927) American civil rights leader; wife of Martin Luther King

28

James Monroe (1758) 5th President of the United States

Harper Lee (1926) American author who wrote *To Kill a Mockingbird*

29

Duke Ellington (1899) American jazz composer, pianist, and bandleader

Oliver Ellsworth (1745) Chief justice, U.S. Supreme Court.

30

Mary II (1662) queen of England, Scotland, and Ireland

Juliana (1909) queen of the Netherlands from 1948 until 1980

The "opening" month

April is the fourth month of the year. It has thirty days. In ancient Roman times, when the year began in March, April was the second month of the year.

The Romans called this month *Aprilis.* The name comes from a Latin word that means "to open." In the northern part of the world, April usually brings more changes than any other month. The last ice and snow disappear. The grass turns green. And the buds of trees, shrubs, and flowers begin to open. Small animals are up and about. Birds are singing and building nests.

Long ago, people living in England named this month for their goddess of spring. Her name was Ostra or Eostre. So they called this month *Oster-monath* or *Eostur-monath.* The Christian festival of Easter probably got its name from this goddess.

"April fool!"

There's a spot on your nose!

Did you look to see? If you did, April fool! The joke is on you.

If you have a trick played on you in the United States, you are an "April fool." In England, you might be called a "noddy," which means a "fool" or "simpleton." But if you live in England, don't try to play any tricks in the afternoon of All Fools' Day. In England, tricks are played only till noon. If you do try to play a trick in the afternoon, you will probably hear this shout:

> "Up the ladder and down the wall,
> You're the greatest fool of all!"

In Scotland, a person who is fooled by being sent on some foolish errand—such as finding a left-handed monkey wrench—is said

to be "hunting the gowk." Gowk means "cuckoo" or "simpleton."

And in France, a person who is fooled is called a *poisson d'Avril,* which means "April fish." Why a "fish"? No one is quite sure. Perhaps it is because in April fish are young and easily caught. In France, as a special treat, you can buy chocolate fish on April Fools' Day.

The custom of playing harmless tricks on April 1 is said to have begun in France more than four hundred years ago. At that time, New Year's Day was March 25. Celebrations went on through April 1, at which time people exchanged New Year's gifts.

Then, the French adopted a new calendar. New Year's Day was switched from March 25 to January 1. This confused many people for a long time. On April 1, those who remembered the switch began to play tricks on those who forgot.

Birthday of Buddha
April 8

The Wise One

Buddha is the title people have given to the founder of Buddhism—one of the world's largest religions. The title Buddha means "Wise One" or "Enlightened One."

In Japan, the followers of Buddha celebrate his birthday on April 8. On that day, in hundreds of Buddhist temples, children stand in line. Slowly, they approach a tiny, open shrine covered with flowers. Inside the shrine is a statue of the baby Buddha.

One by one, in turn, each child takes a small ladle and pours a little sweet tea over the statue. Why? This is the way the children show their love for Buddha.

This day is also known as the Flower Festival, because it is the time of year when cherry trees begin to blossom.

Japanese children honor Buddha on his birthday.

Festival of freedom

Long ago, the Jewish people were slaves in Egypt. God knew that the Jews longed to be free. To help the Jews, He chose one of them, a man named Moses. God appeared to Moses and told him that he was to lead his people to freedom. God then told Moses what must be done.

Moses ordered his people to do as God had said. Each family was to mark its doorway with the blood of a lamb. The people were to stay in their houses. They were to gather their belongings together and be ready to leave Egypt.

During the night, the Angel of Death visited every Egyptian home. And in each home, the first-born child died. But the Jews were safe. The Angel of Death saw the blood on their doorways and went by, or passed over, their houses. This is how the Jewish feast called Passover got its name.

After this terrible night, the Egyptian king, or pharaoh, let the Jews go. Afraid that the pharaoh might change his mind, the Jews left in a hurry. They did not even have time to

bake their daily bread. They just wrapped up the dough and took it with them.

When the Jews did stop to eat, they baked the dough over fires. But the dough had no leaven, or yeast, in it. This kind of bread, which is like a cracker, is called unleavened bread. And this is why Passover is also known as the Feast of Unleavened Bread.

Today, Passover begins with the Seder (SAY duhr), which is both a religious service and a feast. The family prays and eats traditional foods. One of these foods is matzah, which is an unleavened bread. After the Seder, everyone sings happy folksongs.

Jews have celebrated Passover for more than three thousand years. This freedom festival begins on the fifteenth day of the Hebrew month of Nisan, which is in March or April. It lasts for seven or eight days.

At Passover, Jewish families gather for the Seder. On the table are traditional foods and an extra glass of wine called Elijah's cup. This wine is poured in honor of the prophet Elijah.

He is risen!

Jesus Christ died on a cross on a Friday almost two thousand years ago. Christians believe that on the following Sunday Christ arose from the dead and, in so doing, proved that He is the Son of God. The day Jesus died and was buried is known as Good Friday. The following Sunday is Easter.

Christians celebrate this joyful holy day by going to church. Special Easter services are held outdoors at sunrise. As Easter dawns, the people pray, sing hymns, and listen to music.

Most Christians celebrate Easter between March 22 and April 25. Others celebrate it between April 3 and May 8. But, whenever Easter comes, it's the oldest, the most important, and the most joyful of all Christian holy days.

Bunnies and bells

Who brings colored eggs at Easter? It all depends on where you live.

Children in the United States and Canada say the Easter bunny, or rabbit, brings eggs at Easter. Children in England and Germany say the hare brings colored eggs at Easter. A hare looks like a rabbit, but it's larger, with longer ears and legs. The legend about the hare and colored Easter eggs began in Germany.

In Italy, Belgium, and France, children say Easter eggs are brought by the church bells. There, church bells do not ring from Good Friday until Easter Sunday. Because of this, people say that the bells have flown off to Rome. As the bells fly back home for Easter, they drop colored eggs for boys and girls to find.

Where did the custom of coloring Easter eggs come from? No one knows for sure. The ancient Egyptians dyed colored eggs for their friends. So did the ancient Chinese, Greeks, and Persians.

Not all Easter eggs are real eggs. Many are made of wood, paper, glass, and other material. A favorite of children is made of sugar. The large sugar egg has a peephole. Inside the egg you see a scene like the one described in the story on page 150.

Children play games with Easter eggs. They roll eggs down a hill to see how many

The beautiful designs on these Ukrainian Easter eggs were painted by hand.

143

These girls, dressed in their colorful Ukrainian costumes, are dyeing and decorating Easter eggs.

eggs can make it and not crack. A famous Easter Egg Roll is held on the White House lawn in Washington, D.C.

Rolling Easter eggs is fun, and so is eating them. But there are more foods than eggs to enjoy on Easter. Lamb is an Easter favorite in many countries. In Greece, it is served with a jam made of rose petals.

People in Russia eat an Easter bread that is full of plump white raisins and tastes like cake. In some countries of Eastern Europe, people enjoy an Easter cake shaped like a skirt. It is called *babka,* which means "little old woman." Easter cakes in Italy are shaped like a rabbit, which is a symbol of birth and new life.

In many countries, people bake Easter cookies and cakes shaped like a lamb. A lamb has long been a symbol of Jesus. Hot cross buns are another favorite food. These are buns with an icing in the shape of a cross. The cross is another important Easter symbol.

Next to food, new clothes are important for Easter. This custom may come from early Christians who wore white robes when received into the Church at this time.

On Easter Sunday, people often wear new clothes to church. After the service, they may stroll down the street in their new hats and outfits. They're part of what is called an "Easter parade."

A real parade is held on Easter in St. Augustine, Florida. It's called "Parade of the Horses and Carriages." There are men in armor on horseback, and people in costume in carriages pulled by horses. The horses wear fancy Easter bonnets. This parade is part of an Easter Festival that lasts for two weeks.

Easter festivals go back to ancient times. At first, the festivities celebrated the coming of spring. In northern Europe, the goddess of spring was Eostre. Some people say that Easter may have gotten its name from this goddess.

The "Parade of the Horses and Carriages" takes place each Easter in the city of St. Augustine, Florida.

Color and decorate your own Easter eggs

To make colored eggs, start with white hard-cooked eggs. Ask a grown-up to cook them for you. Then cover your work space with a pad of newspaper.

To make the dye solution, add a teaspoonful of vinegar to half a cupful of warm tap water. Drop in 20 drops of food coloring and stir. Do the same for each color. If you have Easter egg dye from the store, follow the directions on the package.

To color an egg, put it on a spoon and lower it into the dye solution. Leave it in until it is the shade you want.

To shine your colored eggs, rub them with a cloth dipped in vegetable oil or shortening.

Your Easter eggs don't all have to be solid colors. You can dye some of them so that they have swirls of color such as you see in some marbles.

Add a teaspoonful of salad oil to your dye mixture. Mix the oil in well. Keep the egg in the dye for a few minutes.

When you lift it out, it will have beautiful swirls of color.

Would you like to have colored eggs with designs on them? One way is to draw a design on an egg with a crayon before you dye the egg. When you take the egg out of the dye, the design will show through.

Or, wrap string or rubber bands around an egg. After the egg is colored, take off the wrapping and you'll see a design.

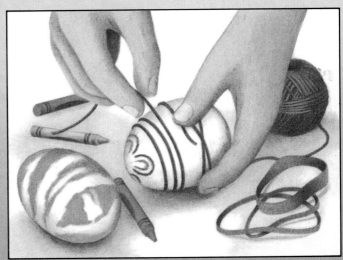

You can make this Easter bunny with a colored egg.

For the eyes, cut out two round pieces of white paper. Draw a dot in each eye. A button makes a good nose. For whiskers, use strips of white paper. Cut out the ears from construction paper. Glue all of these in place.

To make the holder, use a strip of construction paper. All you have to do is tape the ends together.

The Sugar Egg

by Carolyn Sherwin Bailey

There was a very important proclamation on the gate of the king's palace, and this was what it said:

"The king wishes a new and different kind of Easter egg for the prince and the princess. It must be brought to the palace on Easter Eve, and there will be a prize for it if it pleases their royal highnesses. If it is like all the former Easter eggs, the subject who brings it will be banished."

Now whoever heard of anything so absurd? Everyone in the kingdom, down to the most humble subject, knew their royal highnesses, the Prince Particular and the Princess Perhaps. Not that those were their real names, but whenever the prince was asked if he liked a new toy or game, he would say, "Oh, not particularly," and then he would turn up his nose.

And if you asked the princess if she would like to play something quite merry, she was very apt to say, "Oh, perhaps," with a toss of her head, which meant that she did not care whether she did or not.

Of course, every Easter in the past, their royal highnesses had hunted for colored eggs on the palace grounds, and had large chocolate eggs made for them in the palace kitchen, and eaten the pheasants' eggs for breakfast on Easter Day. How, in the entire kingdom, would it be possible to hatch a new and different egg for them? It could not be done. All the hens hung their heads in despair, and all the farmers expected to be banished from the kingdom on Easter Monday.

But it was not a place of giving up, and in spite of their being so hard to please, their subjects loved the Prince Particular and the Princess Perhaps. So whoever read that strange proclamation on the palace gate went home with the wish to find just the kind of Easter egg for which the king had asked. And a great many people went to work trying to make one.

It was funny, though, the way in which they went about it.

There was the baker. He decided to put several dozen eggs into a huge, egg-shaped cake, so he whisked them up as light as foam, mixed them with flour and other good things, and made a great cake which he frosted with white to look like the biggest egg ever made. On top he put the royal crest in yellow icing. But what a very indigestible Easter egg this one was!

And there was the toy man. He made a mammoth egg-shaped toy dirigible of white rubber, and large enough for their royal highnesses to take a short trip over the palace

treetops and as far as the sea. It was just like a giant egg, but so costly and made with such pains that the toy man had to neglect carving the little wooden dolls and animals which the peasant boys and girls loved so much to buy at his shop.

There also was the jewel cutter. He cut two clear, white diamonds in the shape of tiny eggs, one for the prince to wear as a pin in his scarf, and the other for the princess to hang on a golden chain about her neck. But they only sparkled and sent out darts of light; to touch, they were as cold as the winter that had just passed.

So on Easter Eve there was a crowd of the king's subjects at the entrance to the palace, each with his or her odd Easter egg. They were carved of wood, and shaped of gold and silver, painted in all the colors of the rainbow, and some of them so large that they had to be drawn in carts up to the gates.

And on the edge of the crowd came Mother Joy, who lived all alone in a tiny cottage on the border of the forest. She had very little

comfort of her own, but all the children knew
and loved her. Such barley sugar candy sticks
as Mother Joy made for them, and she could
show them the first young magpies, the first
cowslips, and where the fresh cress grew in
the brook! But, in spite of this, it was strange
that Mother Joy should be here at the gate of
the palace on Easter Eve, so poor, and so old.
And when people spoke of it, Mother Joy only
smiled an odd smile and hid something in her
apron.

So all the new and different eggs were taken
into the palace throne room to be judged, while
the subjects waited outside. But the egg balloon
had to be tied to the palace chimney, and
everyone was sure that it would take the prize.
They waited and waited. Then, suddenly, there
came the sound of their royal highnesses
laughing more merrily than they ever had
before, and everyone was called in to see the
prizegiving.

Such a surprise! On a purple velvet pillow
in the lap of the king, the prince and princess
and all the court crowded around it, was a little
hollow sugar egg. It had a piece of glass fitted
in the end like a fairy window, and inside, made
of scraps of colored tissue paper and lace and
grasses, there was a wee house, a green

meadow with flowers and children at play in it. Spring, as it comes in the country, was there inside the little sugar egg, seen through the fairy window in the end.

"The prizewinning egg!" cried the king, holding up the sugar egg. "Their royal highnesses have never been so happy in their lives with any Easter egg before. They want to go right out into the fields and play. Riches and a coronet for the maker!"

And Mother Joy in her apron came up to the throne, for she had known what to bring to the palace on Easter Eve; that little picture of spring, with a fairy window to see it through.

It happened that all the eggs won prizes of one sort and another. But the best of all was the little sugar egg. They became the fashion in the kingdom, and we have had them ever since.

"The British are coming!"

By the rude bridge that arched the flood,
   Their flag to April's breeze unfurled,
Here once the embattled farmers stood,
   And fired the shot heard round the world.

from *Concord Hymn*
by Ralph Waldo Emerson

A patriot is a person who loves his or her country. The patriots of the American colonies felt this way. But they were being treated unfairly by the British. The chance of war grew greater each day.

The patriots of Massachusetts began to build up war supplies in Concord, a town near Boston.

British troops in Boston were alerted. The soldiers—known as redcoats because of their red jackets—got their orders. Destroy the supplies in Concord!

On the night of April 18, 1775, two things happened. The redcoats left Boston for Concord. And Paul Revere, a Boston patriot, rode through the countryside, shouting the warning, "The British are coming!"

Early next morning, the redcoats marched into Lexington, where they were surprised by minutemen—trained men ready to fight in a minute's notice. The first shots in the American Revolutionary War were fired. Nobody knows who fired the first shot. The first brave patriots died.

British redcoats and American patriots fought the second battle of the American Revolution at North Bridge in Concord, Massachusetts.

Again the redcoats were met by fighting patriots at Concord. The patriots stormed North Bridge outside of town. More shots rang out and more blood was shed.

The redcoats were forced to withdraw. And all the way back to Boston, there was a running battle with more patriots. Paul Revere's warning the night before had stirred up a lot of people.

The midnight ride of Paul Revere is staged every year in Massachusetts on the third Monday in April. It's Patriots' Day, the anniversary of the start of the Revolutionary War in America.

Patriots' Day is also a holiday in Maine, another state that gave many patriots in America's fight for freedom.

A holiday for trees

Arbor Day

Whoever heard of a holiday for trees? You have—if you've heard of Arbor Day. *Arbor* is another word for tree. On Arbor Day, many people—especially schoolchildren—plant trees.

Most states in the United States, and most of the provinces in Canada, celebrate Arbor Day. Many other countries also have days or weeks for planting trees.

The first Arbor Day in the United States was on April 10, 1872, in Nebraska. It was the idea of J. Sterling Morton. Morton, a newspaperman, knew how important trees are to the land. Trees enrich the soil and help to keep water on it. The state offered prizes to the groups and people who planted the most trees. On that first Arbor Day, Nebraskans planted more than a million trees.

After Morton died, Nebraska changed the date of Arbor Day to his birthday, April 22. California celebrates Arbor Day on March 7, the birthday of Luther Burbank. The people in California honor Burbank because he developed many new kinds of trees and plants, such as the Santa Rosa plum, the Burbank potato, and the Shasta daisy.

The people of Israel also have an arbor day. It is in the spring and is called *Tu B'Shebat* (TOO buh shuh VAT), which means "the fifteenth day (of the Hebrew month) of Shebat." This day is also known as the New Year for Trees.

St. George's Day
April 23

The dragon slayer

The princess wept and trembled with fear as the huge, horrible dragon came toward her. She closed her eyes and prayed for the terror to end quickly. She didn't want to die. But only by sacrificing herself to the monster could she save the people of her father's kingdom. If the dragon ate her, it would leave them alone.

Suddenly a knight in silver armor rode out of the nearby forest. Drawing a gleaming sword, he spurred his horse into a gallop. Straight at the dragon he charged!

The dragon gave an ear-splitting snarl and rose on its hind legs. It towered over the horseman, but he did not stop. With a single

blow of his sword, he cut off the monster's head! The princess and her people were saved—by the brave knight, Saint George!

No one knows how the legend of Saint George and the dragon got started. Saint George was a real man. He was a Roman soldier. But he certainly never killed a dragon. He was also a Christian. And because he refused to give up his religion, he was put to death. He died on April 23, 303, which is why this date is now St. George's Day.

Many stories, such as the one about the slaying of the dragon, were made up about him. Because of these stories, he became very popular. In 1350 he was made the patron, or protecting, saint of England. English knights and soldiers often wore a red cross on a white background on their shields or clothing. This was called the cross of Saint George. It appears on the flag of England and on the British Union flag.

Simpson and his donkey

The air crackled with the sound of rifle and machine gun fire. The earth shuddered from the explosions of cannon shells. Through this storm of death, thousands of soldiers streamed up a long stretch of beach toward distant hills.

It was April 25, 1915—early in World War I. The soldiers were men of the Australian and New Zealand Army Corps, called Anzacs for short. They were invading Gallipoli, a long neck of land that sticks out from the coast of Turkey.

One of the Anzacs was John Simpson Kirkpatrick, known to his friends as "Simpson." Simpson's duty was to find wounded soldiers and bring them to safety.

One day, shortly after the landing, Simpson saw a donkey wandering about. It was one of a number of donkeys used to carry water. This one had lost its driver. Simpson realized the donkey could be of great help in carrying wounded men. He took the animal with him.

Each day, Simpson led the donkey, which he named "Duffy," out to search for the wounded. The man and animal, risking their lives to save others, became a familiar sight. But on May 19, Simpson's luck ran out. He was killed. Duffy came back alone.

The story of Simpson and his donkey became a famous tale of World War I. After

the war, a statue of Simpson and Duffy was
put up in Melbourne, Australia, where
Simpson had lived.

April 25, the day the Anzacs landed at
Gallipoli, became known as Anzac Day. It is a
national holiday in Australia and New
Zealand. There are sunrise services at war
memorials and military parades. This day
honors the memory of those who died at
Gallipoli and in all battles since then. And on
Anzac Day, a wreath of flowers is placed at
the statue of Simpson and his donkey.

A Confederate hero

The American Civil War was a bitter struggle between the North and the South. The war lasted four long years. In that time, more than half a million men died.

At the start of the war, in 1861, a young Tennessee farm boy named Sam Davis joined the Confederate, or Southern, army. He was nineteen years old. Two years later, Sam was an experienced army scout. It was his job to get information about the enemy.

One day, in 1863, Sam and a number of other scouts were on their way back with secret information. Near Pulaski, Tennessee, they were captured by Northern troops. The scouts were searched. At first, nothing was found. Then, secret papers were discovered in Sam's boots. Looking further, the Northern soldiers cut open Sam's saddle. More secret information was found.

Sam was in uniform, so he knew he should be held as a prisoner of war. Instead, he was tried as a spy and sentenced to be hanged. Sam was offered the chance to save his life—

if he would tell who gave him the secret
information. But he refused.

"I would rather die a thousand deaths,"
young Sam said, "than betray a friend or be
false to duty." These were Sam's last words.

Sam Davis and all the Civil War dead of
the South are honored on Confederate
Memorial Day. Most Southern states observe
this holiday. Some states celebrate it in April,
and some at other times of the year.

May

1

Mother (Mary) Jones (1830) labor leader of Appalachian coal miners

M. Scott Carpenter (1925) American astronaut and oceanographer

2

Catherine the Great (1729) German princess who became empress of Russia

Bing Crosby (1904) American singer

3

Golda Meir (1898) prime minister of Israel

Pete Seeger (1919) American folk singer and composer

4

Horace Mann (1796) American educator

Thomas Huxley (1825) English biologist

Who shares my birthday?

Is your birthday in May? The names of some of the famous people born in May are shown on the calendar on this page and the next. What do you know about the person who shares your birthday?

5

Karl Marx (1818) German philosopher, revolutionary, and writer

Nellie Bly (1867?) American newspaper reporter (real name Elizabeth Cochrane)

6

Robert E. Peary (1856) American who discovered the North Pole

Willie Mays (1931) American baseball player; third greatest home run hitter

7

Robert Browning (1812) English poet

John Unitas (1933) American who became one of the greatest football quarterbacks

8

Harry S. Truman (1884) 33rd President of the United States

Fulton J. Sheen (1895) American religious leader

9

John Brown (1800) American antislavery reformer

Sir James Barrie (1860) Scottish author who wrote *Peter Pan*

10

Fred Astaire (1899) American entertainer

Ella Tambussi Grasso (1919) first woman governor of Connecticut

11

Ottmar Mergenthaler (1854) German-American inventor of Linotype (a machine that sets metal type)

Irving Berlin (1888) American songwriter

12

Florence Nightingale (1820) English nurse; founded modern professional nursing

Yogi Berra (1925) American baseball player and manager

13

Maria Theresa (1717) Austrian empress

Joe Louis (1914) the "Brown Bomber," American boxing champion

14

Gabriel Fahrenheit (1686) German scientist; developed the Fahrenheit temperature scale

15

L. Frank Baum (1856) American author of *Oz* books

Pierre Curie (1859) French scientist who, with his wife, Marie, discovered radium

16

William Seward (1801) American statesman who purchased Alaska from Russia

Olga Korbut (1955) Soviet Olympic gold medal gymnast

17

Edward Jenner (1749) English doctor; discovered vaccination against smallpox

Alfonso XIII (1886) king of Spain

18

Bertrand Russell (1872) British philosopher and mathematician

Dame Margot Fonteyn (1919) British ballerina

19

Dame Nellie Melba (1861) Australian opera singer

Lorraine Hansberry (1930) American playwright who wrote *A Raisin in the Sun*

20

Antoinette Blackwell (1825) first ordained woman minister in U.S.

Sigrid Undset (1882) Norwegian author who won a Nobel Prize

21

Elisha Root (1808) American mechanic and inventor

Glenn Hammond Curtiss (1879) American aviator and aeronautical inventor

22

Richard Wagner (1813) German musical composer

Arthur Conan Doyle (1859) British author of the Sherlock Holmes stories

23

Carolus Linnaeus (1707) Swedish botanist

Mary Cassatt (1845) American painter best known for pictures of mothers and children

24

Victoria (1819) British queen who ruled for 63 years

Jane Byrne (1934) American politician; first woman mayor of Chicago

25

Ralph Waldo Emerson (1803) American writer

Beverly Sills (1929) American singer

26

Sally Ride (1951) American astronaut; first American woman in space

John Wayne (1907) American movie actor

27

Julia Ward Howe (1819) American poet; wrote "The Battle Hymn of the Republic"

Rachel Carson (1907) American biologist who wrote *The Sea Around Us*

28

Jim Thorpe (1888) American Indian who was a great athlete

Patrick White (1912) Australian author who won a Nobel Prize

29

Patrick Henry (1736) American patriot

John F. Kennedy (1917) 35th President of the United States

30

Rosa Raisa (1893) Polish-born opera singer

Benny Goodman (1909) American clarinetist and bandleader

31

Walt Whitman (1819) American poet; wrote *Leaves of Grass*

Elizabeth Coatsworth (1893) American author of books for children

The month of Maia

May is the fifth month of the year. It has thirty-one days. In early Roman times, when the year began in March, May was the third month of the year.

There are several stories about how this month was named. According to one story, May was named for *Maia*, the Roman goddess of spring and growth. Another story has it that May is short for *majores*, a Latin word that means "older men." Some people think that the Romans held May sacred to older men and that June was sacred to the *juniores*, or young men.

People living in England long ago called this month *Thrimilce*. This means "to milk three times." At this time of year, there was much new grass. Cows had more to eat and gave more milk. So they could be milked three times a day, instead of twice a day.

Maypoles
and parades

In many countries, the first of May is May Day—a day to welcome spring. People gather flowers and dance, often around a Maypole.

May Day came to the United States from England—but it was brought to England by the ancient Romans. In Rome, there was a day in spring when the young men paraded through the city, carrying a pine tree. There was also a festival to honor Flora, the Roman goddess of flowers. When the Romans conquered England, the pine tree became a Maypole.

On May Day in England, the pole was set up on the village green and decorated with flowers and ribbons. A May Queen was picked and crowned with flowers. Villagers danced around the Maypole, holding the ends of ribbons that hung from the pole. As they danced, they wove the ribbons in and out.

In time, some people thought the merrymakers worshiped the Maypole. For a while, the Maypole was forbidden by law. But it reappeared later. To this day, children in parts of England and elsewhere still sing and dance around the Maypole on May Day.

In some countries, the first of May is Labor Day, a holiday in honor of working people. And in some Communist countries, it is a day

Children in England dance around a Maypole on May Day.

to honor the nation. People listen to speeches and watch parades of weapons and soldiers that show the country's strength.

In Russia and some other countries, Communist governments have changed to other kinds of governments. May Day has changed, too. There are parades and speeches, but there are also parties with singers, dancers, and acrobats in honor of May.

Fly a fish!

May 5 is a double holiday in Japan. It is Children's Day, which has been a national holiday since 1948. It is also Boys' Day, a festival that is hundreds of years old.

On this day, families with one or more sons raise a bamboo pole on their roof or in their yard. On the pole fly hollow cloth or paper streamers shaped like the kind of fish called a carp. The carp is a symbol of strength, courage, and determination. The largest fish streamer, which is at the top of the pole, stands for the oldest son. The shortest streamer is for the youngest son.

Many families display things that remind boys of strength and of the past. Groups of tiny dolls show scenes and characters based on Japanese hero stories. Small images of Japanese generals hold swords or spears.

Families may also put out armor, helmets, and other equipment once used by family members. Some families even hang up a silk banner that has on it the family emblem.

On Boys' Day, boys often bathe in water in which the sword-shaped leaves of the iris plant have been soaked. These leaves are another symbol of strength. And for strength and good luck, boys eat rice wrapped in leaves of iris, bamboo, and oak.

Some years ago, the Japanese government made this day a new national holiday called Children's Day to honor both boys and girls.

*This painting in a Mexico City museum shows the
Mexicans defeating the French in the Battle of Puebla.*

The Battle of Puebla

A little more than a hundred years ago, France started a war with Mexico. In the Mexican city of Puebla, two forts blocked the advance of some six thousand French troops. The forts were manned by two thousand Mexican soldiers under the command of General Ignacio Zaragoza.

On May 5, 1862, cannons boomed and rifle shots rang out as the French soldiers attacked the two forts. Before the day was over, one fort was in ruins and more than a thousand French soldiers lay dead. The Mexicans had won the battle.

The battlefield is now a city park. In the park, there's a statue of General Zaragoza on horseback. Near the statue is a war museum that was one of the forts that Zaragoza and his men defended.

In the museum is a display of hundreds of toy soldiers set up to show what happened that day. Mexicans call the day *Cinco de Mayo*, which is Spanish for "fifth of May." *Cinco de Mayo* is a national holiday in Mexico.

For someone I love

Even though you can show how much you love your mother on any day, a special day is set aside to honor mothers.

In the United States, Canada, and Australia, Mother's Day is the second Sunday in May. This special day was first observed in the United States in 1908 through the efforts of Anna Jarvis.

On Mother's Day, some mothers get cards and gifts that their children have made for them. Other mothers might get candy or flowers. Many women wear carnations on Mother's Day. If a woman wears colored carnations, it means her mother is living. If she wears white carnations, it means that her mother has died.

People in England celebrate a special day called Mothering Sunday. It comes about three weeks before Easter. On that day, sons and daughters living away from home come home with flowers and special cakes or candy for their mothers. Some children give their mothers flowers that are blessed in church on Mothering Sunday.

What about fathers? Do they have a special day, too? Of course, they do. Fathers get cards and gifts their children have made for them, as well as neckties and other gifts. Father's Day is celebrated in June in the United States, Canada, and England and in September in Australia.

My Mother Is the Most Beautiful Woman in the World

A Russian folk tale retold by Becky Reyher

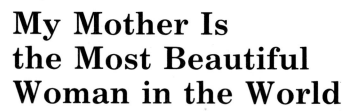

Once upon a time, long, long ago, when the harvest season had come again in the Ukraine, the villagers were all busy cutting and gathering the wheat. For this is the land from which most Russians get the flour for their bread.

Marfa and Ivan went to the field early each day, as did all their children. There they stayed until sundown. Varya was Marfa's and Ivan's youngest little girl, six years old. When everyone went to the fields in harvest time, Varya went, too. Her legs were so short she had to run and skip to keep up with her mother's and father's long steps.

"Varyachka, you are a little slowpoke!" her father said to her. Then, laughing loudly, he swung her up on his shoulder where she had to hold tight to his neck, for his arms were full carrying the day's lunch and the long scythe to cut the wheat.

In the field, in the long even rows between the thick wheat, Varya knew just what she must do. First, she must stay at least twenty or thirty paces behind her father, who now took even greater and bigger steps, so that he might have plenty of room to swing wide the newly sharpened scythe.

"Stand back, Varyachka! Mind the scythe!" he warned. Swish, swish, swish, went his even strokes, and down came the wheat, faster and faster, as he made his great strides.

Soon Marfa began to follow Ivan. She gathered the wheat in sheaves or bunches just big enough to bind together with a strand of braided wheat. Varya, eager to be useful, helped gather the wheat, and held each bunch while her mother tied it. When three sheaves were tied, they were stacked against each other in a little pyramid.

"Careful, Varyachka!" her mother cautioned. "The wheat side up!"

After a while, instead of long rows of wheat, there were long rows of sheaves, standing stiffly.

Sometimes Varya forgot to follow her mother. On very hot days she stopped to rest upon the warm ground, and let her tired, bare feet and toes tickle the dark, moist earth. A while later she ran and caught up with her mother, and then her mother hugged her to her and wiped her dripping face. Even though her mother's arms and bosom were hot and damp, they felt cool and restful to Varya.

Day after day, Ivan, Marfa, and Varya went
to the field to cut and stack the wheat. Then
a big wagon came and everyone pitched the
wheat up to the driver, who packed it in solidly
and carefully and took it to the threshing barn.

The villagers worked tirelessly. Their
muscles ached, but there was a song in their
hearts, and there were merry chuckles on their
lips. Hard work produced a rich harvest. There
would be wheat for everybody.

Finally, it was the last day of the harvest.
By evening, all the wheat would be cut, stacked
in pyramids, and waiting for the wagon to take
it to the threshing barn.

Bright and early, Marfa, Ivan, and Varya
went to the wheat field. "We must get to it,"
warned Ivan. "This is our last day to get the
wheat in!"

"It has been a good crop, Ivan, hasn't it?"
asked Marfa.

"Indeed, yes!" Ivan answered heartily. "And
it will mean plenty to eat for the winter. We
have much to be thankful for."

Marfa and Ivan worked quicker and harder
than ever. They did not seem to notice the hot
sun. The wheat swished almost savagely as it
came rushing down.

But to Varya the day seemed the longest she
had ever lived. The sun seemed hotter than on
any other day, and her feet seemed almost too
heavy to lift.

Varya peered into the next row of wheat that
was not yet cut. There it was cool and pleasant
and the sun did not bear down with its almost

unbearable heat. Varya moved in just a little
farther to surround herself with that blessed
coolness. "How lucky I am!" she thought, "to
be able to hide away from the hot sun. I will
do this for just a few minutes. Surely,
Mamochka will not mind if I do not help her
all the day."

Soon Varya grew sleepy, for in so cool a place
one could curl up and be very quiet and
comfortable.

When Varya woke, she jumped to her feet
and started to run toward her mother. But her
mother was nowhere in sight.

Varya called, "Mama! Mama! Mamochka!"
But there was no answer.

Sometimes her mother got ahead of her and was so busy with her work she did not hear. "Maybe if I run along the row, I will catch up with her," Varya thought. She ran and ran, and soon she was out of breath, but nowhere could she see her mother.

"Maybe I have gone in the wrong direction," she said to herself. So she ran the other way. But here, too, there was no trace of her mother.

Varya was alone in the wheat fields. She could see nothing but tall pyramids of wheat towering above her. When she called out, her voice brought no response, no help. Overhead, the sun was not so bright as it had been. Varya knew that soon it would be night and that she must find her mother.

Varya pushed through the last of the wheat that had not yet been cut, breaking her own pathway, which bent and hurt the wheat. She would not have done this had she not been frightened.

It was almost dark when Varya stumbled into a clearing where several men and women had paused to gossip after the day's work. It took her only a second to see that these were strangers, and that neither her mother nor father were among them.

The little girl stared ahead of her, not knowing what to do. One of the men spied her and said in a booming voice he thought was friendly, "Look what we have here!"

Everyone turned to Varya. She was sorry that with so many strangers looking at her she had her hair caught back in a tiny braid with a bit of string, and that she was wearing her oldest, most faded dress. Surely, too, by now her face must be as streaked with dirt as were her legs and dress. This made her burst into tears.

"Poor little thing," cried one of the women, putting her arms around Varya. "She is lost!" But this sympathy, and the strange voices, made Varya want her mother all the more. She could not help crying.

"We must know her name, and the name of her mother and father. Then we can unite them," said the women.

"Little girl, little girl," they said, "what is your name? What is your mother and father's name?" But Varya was too unhappy to speak.

Finally, because her longing for her mother was so great, she sobbed out:

"My mother is the most beautiful woman in the world!"

All the men and women smiled. The tallest man, Kolya, clapped his hands and laughingly said, "Now we have something to go on. Bring Katya, Manya, Vyera, Nadya," the tall man, Kolya, called to one boy. "And don't forget the beauty, Lisa," he called to another boy.

The women came running. These were orders from Kolya, the village leader. Also, the mothers who had left the fields early to get supper for their families thought perhaps this was their child who was lost.

As each beautiful woman came rushing up, blushing and proud that she had been so chosen, Kolya would say to her: "We have a little lost

one here. Stand back, everyone, while the little one tells us if this is her mother!"

The mothers laughed and pushed, and called to Kolya: "You big tease! What about asking each mother if this is her child? We know our children!"

To Varya this was very serious, for she was lost and she was desperate without her mother. As she looked at each strange woman, Varya shook her head in disappointment and sobbed harder. Soon every known beauty from far and near, from distances much farther than a child could have strayed, had come and gone. Not one of them was Varya's mother.

The villagers were really worried. They shook their heads. Kolya spoke for them. "One of us will have to take the little one home for the night. Tomorrow may bring fresh wisdom to guide us."

Just then a breathless, excited woman came puffing up to the crowd. Her face was big and broad, and her body even larger. Her eyes were little pale slits between a great lump of a nose. The mouth was almost toothless. Even when she was a young girl everyone had said, "A homely girl like Marfa is lucky to get a good husband like Ivan."

"Varyachka!" cried this woman.

"Mamochka!" cried the little girl, and they fell into each other's arms. The two of them beamed upon each other. The smile Varya had longed for was once again shining upon her. Varya cuddled into that ample and familiar bosom.

All of the villagers smiled thankfully when
Varya looked up from her mother's shoulder
and said with joy:

"This is my mother! I told you my mother
is the most beautiful woman in the world!"

The group of friends and neighbors, too,
beamed upon each other. Kolya repeated the
proverb so well known to all of them, a proverb
which little Varya had just proved: "We do not
love people because they are beautiful, but they
seem beautiful to us because we love them."

Birthday for two queens

The Monday before May 25 is a national holiday in Canada. That's when Canadians celebrate the birthdays of two British queens born more than a hundred years apart.

The first queen was Queen Victoria. She was born May 24, 1819. During her long life, her birthday came to have a special meaning. The holiday is named in her honor.

The second queen is Queen Elizabeth II, who is now the British queen. She was born April 21, 1926. In Canada, her official birthday is observed on Victoria Day.

But in the United Kingdom, Australia, and other countries that live under British law, the official birthday of the queen is celebrated in early June.

Queen Victoria ruled the United Kingdom longer than any other British ruler. Her birthday, long celebrated as Victoria Day, is a holiday throughout Canada.

184

**Jumping Frog
Jubilee**

Jumping frogs!

A frog-jumping contest in California is
famous because of a famous short story. The
story was written by Mark Twain, who also
wrote *The Adventures of Tom Sawyer* and
many other books. He called the story "The
Celebrated Jumping Frog of Calaveras
County."

In Twain's story, two men hold a jumping
contest between their frogs. Usually, a frog
can jump about twenty times the length of its
body. But the loser in the story can't even
get off the ground. Someone had filled the
frog with small bits of lead used in shotgun
shells.

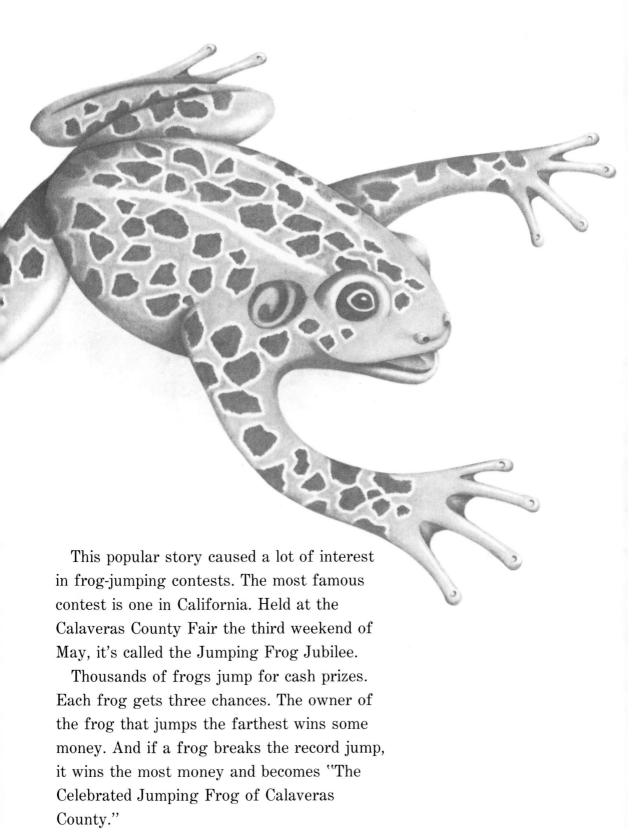

This popular story caused a lot of interest in frog-jumping contests. The most famous contest is one in California. Held at the Calaveras County Fair the third weekend of May, it's called the Jumping Frog Jubilee.

Thousands of frogs jump for cash prizes. Each frog gets three chances. The owner of the frog that jumps the farthest wins some money. And if a frog breaks the record jump, it wins the most money and becomes "The Celebrated Jumping Frog of Calaveras County."

America remembers

Memorial Day honors Americans who died in war. This day is also known as Decoration Day, because graves of the war dead are decorated with flowers and flags.

No one is sure just how or when this day came about. But the first national observance of Memorial Day was May 30, 1868. That was when Major General John A. Logan named May 30 as a day to decorate the graves of Northern soldiers who died in the Civil War.

On Memorial Day, Americans decorate the graves of men and women who served their country in war and peace.

Since then, Memorial Day has become a day to honor all Americans who died in the Civil War and the wars that followed.

After World War I, Memorial Day also became Poppy Day. In France, red poppies grew on battlefields. So, as a reminder, American veterans sold artificial poppies on May 30 to help needy French and Belgian children.

As time went on, the sale of poppies helped needy veterans. Poppy Day is now a day in Poppy Week. This week ends on the Saturday before Memorial Day.

Memorial Day is now observed on May 30 or on the last Monday in May.

Saint Joan of Arc
May 30

The Maid of Orléans

The year is 1429. A young French peasant girl—only seventeen years old—is clad in armor and mounted on a war horse. She holds her sword high in the air. Above her flies the banner of France. Behind her rides the French army, ready for battle. The young girl's name is Jeanne d'Arc.

Joan of Arc, as she is called in English, lived during a time the French and English fought to control France. In her early teens, Joan said she heard voices from heaven. The voices urged her to save France.

At first, people laughed at Joan. A young girl lead men in battle? Impossible! Joan convinced the king to give her command of the French army. Through her military skill and personal bravery, Joan of Arc freed the city of Orléans from the English. Joan defeated the English in four other battles. She was wounded, but went on fighting.

About a year after Joan of Arc first took up the sword, she was captured. The English threw her into prison and then tried her as a witch. On May 30, 1431, the English burned her at the stake in the market place of Rouen.

The Roman Catholic Church declared Joan a saint and honors her on May 30, the day she died. France also remembers this saint and national heroine at other times. One is a holiday in her honor on the second Sunday in May—about the time she led the French army to victory at Orléans and became known forever as the Maid of Orléans.

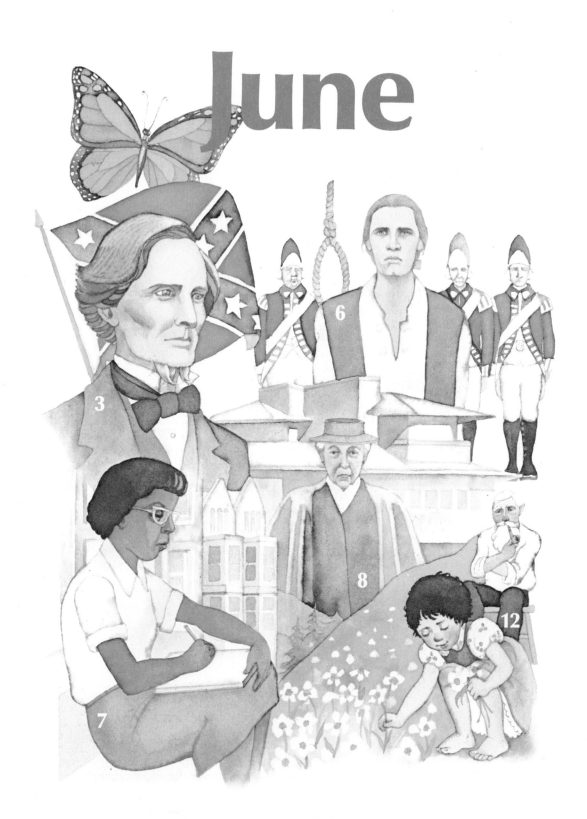

June

1

Brigham Young (1801) American who led the Mormons from Illinois to Utah

Pat Boone (1934) American singer and actor

2

John Randolph of Roanoke (1773) American statesman

Edwin Way Teale (1899) American naturalist, writer, and photographer

3

Jefferson Davis (1808) president of the Confederate States of America

Charles R. Drew (1904) American doctor; set up World War II blood banks

4

George III (1738) king of Great Britain during the American Revolution

Who shares my birthday?

Is your birthday in June? The names of some of the famous people born in June are shown on the calendar on this page and the next. What do you know about the person who shares your birthday?

5

Adam Smith (1723) Scottish economist; wrote *The Wealth of Nations*

John Couch Adams (1819) British astronomer; discovered Neptune

6

Nathan Hale (1755) American patriot hanged as a spy by the British

Thomas Mann (1875) German author who won a Nobel Prize

7

Gwendolyn Brooks (1917) American poet, winner of a Pulitzer Prize, whose poems are about the life of blacks in the city

Nikki Giovanni (1943) American poet

8

Robert Stevenson (1772) Scottish inventor of flashing light in lighthouses

Frank Lloyd Wright (1867) American architect

9

George Stephenson (1781) English inventor, known as "Founder of Railways"

Cole Porter (1893) American composer of popular music

10

Prince Philip (1921) Duke of Edinburgh; husband of Queen Elizabeth

Judy Garland (1922) American singer and movie actress

11

Jeanette Rankin (1880) first woman member of Congress

Jacques-Yves Cousteau (1910) French marine explorer

12

Johanna Spyri (1827) Swiss author of *Heidi*

Anne Frank (1929) Dutch writer, famous for the diary she kept

13

William Butler Yeats (1865) Irish poet

Paavo Nurmi (1897) Finnish long-distance runner

14

Harriet Beecher Stowe (1811) American author of *Uncle Tom's Cabin*

Eric Heiden (1958) American Olympic speed skater

15

Edvard Grieg (1843) Norwegian composer

Ernestine Schumann-Heink (1861) Czech opera singer

16

Arthur Meighen
(1874) a prime
minister of Canada

Katharine Graham
(1917) American
newspaper publisher

17

Charles Gounod
(1818) French
composer of operas

Igor Stravinsky
(1882) Russian-born
composer, famous for
his ballet music

18

Paul McCartney
(1942) English rock
star of the 1960's,
who belonged to a
music group called
the Beatles

19

Lou Gehrig (1903)
American baseball
hero who played
2,130 consecutive
games with the New
York Yankees

20

**Alberto Santos-
Dumont** (1873)
Brazilian aviator and
airplane builder

Lillian Hellman
(1905) American
playwright

21

Daniel C. Beard
(1850) an early leader
of the Boy Scouts of
America

Prince William
(1982) son of Prince
Charles and Princess
Diana of England

22

Julian Huxley
(1887) English
biologist

**Anne Morrow
Lindbergh** (1906)
American author;
wife of Charles
Lindbergh

23

Edward VIII (1894)
English king who
gave up his throne to
marry Wallis
Simpson

Wilma Rudolph
(1940) American
Olympic sprinter

24

E. I. du Pont (1771)
French-born founder
of the world's largest
maker of chemical
products

25

Louis Mountbatten
(1900) British admiral
and World War II
hero

Celia Franca (1921)
British ballet dancer;
founded National
Ballet of Canada

26

Antonia Brica
(1902) first American
woman to conduct
the Berlin Symphony

**Mildred "Babe"
Didrikson Zaharias**
(1914) outstanding
athlete and golfer

27

Peter Paul Rubens
(1577) Flemish
painter

Helen Keller (1880)
famous deaf, blind
American speaker
and author

28

Henry VIII (1491)
king of England

Esther Forbes
(1891) American
author of *Johnny
Tremain* and other
children's books

29

George Goethals
(1858) American
engineer who built
the Panama Canal

George E. Hale
(1868) American
astronomer

30

Lena Horne (1917)
American singer

Czeslaw Milosz
(1919) Polish-born
writer; won the
Nobel Prize for
literature

The month of Juno

June is the sixth month of the year. It has thirty days. In ancient Roman times, when the year began in March, June was the fourth month of the year.

Some people say that June was named for Juno, the Roman goddess of marriage. Others think that the name came from the Latin word *juniores*, meaning "young men." These people say that the Romans held June sacred to young men, just as they held May sacred to the *majores*, or older men.

In the northern half of the world, summer begins on June 20 or 21. In the southern part of the world, this is when winter starts.

Long ago, people in Europe celebrated on Midsummer's Eve, June 23. They built bonfires on the hills and danced far into the night. In Sweden, people still celebrate the coming of summer in this way.

Fifth day, fifth moon

Chinese people in the countries of Malaysia and Taiwan enjoy the Dragon Boat Festival every summer. This celebration comes in the month of the fifth moon on the Chinese calendar—between May 28 and June 28.

More than two thousand years ago, a man named Ch'ü Yüan fell into a river. Ch'ü Yüan was a poet and champion of the people. They loved him very much. When they saw what had happened, they put their boats into the water and raced to rescue him. But his body was never found. Ever since, they have remembered this long-ago race with the Dragon Boat Festival.

The big event of the festival is a colorful
boat race that takes place on the fifth day of
the fifth moon. Each boat is painted like a
dragon, which the Chinese people believe is
the giver of rain.

Onshore, gongs, drums, and horns urge the
rowers in the boats to go faster. The rowers
in each boat follow the rhythm of their
drummer. As the drums beat faster and
faster, the boats skim over the water like
racing dragons—in honor of a poet who died
long ago.

**Shabuot, or
Feast of Weeks**

Day of the Commandments

Shabuot (sha voo oht) is one of the great Jewish festivals. It celebrates the day that God gave the Ten Commandments to Moses, the Jewish leader.

Shabuot is the Hebrew word for "weeks." This festival is also called "Feast of Weeks." This is because it comes seven weeks after the first day of Passover (see page 140).

Long ago, Shabuot was also a harvest festival. It was the time when Jews made a

journey to Jerusalem to make offerings at the
Temple in thanks for their crops. After the
Romans destroyed the Temple, Shabuot
became more and more a time to celebrate
the gift of the Ten Commandments.

Today, Shabuot is when most Reform Jews
celebrate the confirmation of children.
(Orthodox Jewish boys are confirmed on their
thirteenth birthday; girls on their twelfth
birthday.) The ceremony of confirmation is
called bar mitzvah (bahr MIHTS vuh) for boys
and bas (bahs) mitzva for girls. The name
means "son (or daughter) of the
commandment."

Shabuot is celebrated for one or two days.
On the Hebrew calendar (see page 27), this
festival starts on the sixth day of the month
of Sivan, which falls in May or June.

Kamehameha Day
June 11

A feast for a king

statue of Kamehameha I

Today, Hawaii is one of the fifty states of the United States. But two hundred years ago it was a group of islands ruled by many kings. One of the kings, Kamehameha I (kah may hah MAY hah), ruled part of the large island of Hawaii.

Kamehameha was a great warrior. In time, he won control of all the Hawaiian Islands and made them one kingdom. More than a hundred years ago, the last king of Hawaii, Kamehameha V, set aside June 11 as a day to honor his grandfather.

Kamehameha Day is a time for all kinds of festivities. In the city of Honolulu, singers chant songs in front of the statue of the great king. They also decorate the statue with flower wreaths called leis (lays).

After this ceremony, there's a big parade. One float carries a man dressed like the king. He wears a helmet and a cloak of golden feathers. Each of the eight major islands is represented by a princess on horseback.

Later, almost everyone goes to a feast called a luau (LOO ow). The main dish is a whole young pig, roasted for hours in a deep pit. When the roast pig is carried in, the feast—fit for a king—begins!

This rider represents the island of Kauai in the Kamehameha Day parade. Her long wraparound skirt is called a pa'u.

In the King Kamehameha Day parade, Hawaiians play the parts of King Kamehameha and his brave warriors.

Every day during Ramadan, Muslims read their holy book, the Koran.

Ramadan

The long fast

If a person chooses not to eat or drink for a while, he or she "fasts." Muslims—people who follow the Islamic religion—fast for a month every year.

Both the long fast and the month are called Ramadan (ram uh DAHN). This is the ninth month of the Islamic year (see page 28). Because the Islamic calendar is based on the moon, the date of Ramadan changes. In the 1980's in the northern part of the world, Ramadan was observed in the spring. By the year 2000, it will be observed in the winter.

During Ramadan, Muslims fast every day from dawn to sunset. They fast to have their sins forgiven. Those who for some reason cannot fast must make up the days they miss.

In the daytime, Muslims work less and

spend more time praying and reading their
holy book, called the Koran.

A new moon brings an end to Ramadan and
the start of *Id al-Fitr*—"Festival of the
Breaking of the Fast."

This holiday festival may last for several
days. People eat when they please. They often
put on new clothes, visit friends, and exchange
gifts. In Turkey, children know this festival as
the Sugar Festival. It's a time to enjoy rahat
lokoum—Turkish delight—colorful cubes of
gelatin candy covered with powdered sugar.

*During Ramadan, people
in some countries go to
puppet shows at night. The
puppets, made of camel
skin, are worked from
behind a lighted screen.
The people see only the
shadows on the screen.*

The Stars and Stripes

Hats off!
Along the street there comes
A blare of bugles, a ruffle of drums,
A flash of color beneath the sky:
Hats off!
The flag is passing by!

from *The Flag Goes By*
by Henry Holcomb Bennett

The American flag has fifty stars, one for each state in the Union. All fifty states honor the flag on Flag Day. But Flag Day is a holiday in only one state—Pennsylvania.

It was in Pennsylvania, in the city of Philadelphia, that the Continental Congress adopted the first official American flag. The date was June 14, 1777. At that time, the thirteen American colonies were fighting for their liberty. They wanted to be free from Great Britain. As a symbol of their united effort, and their independence, they wanted to have one flag.

When the Revolutionary War started in 1776, Americans fought under many different flags. One flag had a pine tree on it and the words "An Appeal to Heaven." Another had a rattlesnake and the words "Don't Tread on Me." Others had "Liberty or Death" or "Conquer or Die."

The new flag had thirteen stripes—seven red and six white—and thirteen white stars on a field of blue. No one knows who designed this flag or made the first one.

Children dressed in folk costumes proudly carry the Stars and Stripes in the Flag Day parade held in Chicago.

According to one story, the first flag was made by Betsy Ross. It is true that Betsy Ross did sew flags during the Revolutionary War. And she lived in Philadelphia. Her house there is now a national shrine. But there is no proof that she made the first official American flag.

There is no record of why red, white, and blue were chosen as the colors for the flag. But it was said later that the red stands for hardiness and courage, the white for purity and innocence, and the blue for vigilance, perseverance, and justice. The stripes stand for the thirteen original colonies. And there is one star for each state.

Bonfires
and baptisms

Long ago, people in Europe worshiped the
sun. So the return of summer was a time of
great rejoicing. The people lit bonfires—
symbols of the sun—and celebrated all night
and into the next day.

This time was known as Midsummer Eve
(June 23) and Midsummer Day (June 24).
This, of course, is not midsummer—for
summer begins on June 20 or 21. Why it was
called midsummer we can't be sure. Perhaps
it is because this is the time of year when the
sun is at its highest point in the sky and the
days are longest.

Years later, the early Christian church
chose Midsummer Day as the birth date of
Saint John the Baptist. This man has long
been thought of as one of the greatest saints.
It was he who told of the coming of Christ.
He was given the name John the Baptist
because he baptized people—including Jesus.

People in many Christian countries have
celebrated St. John's Day for hundreds of
years. These celebrations are a curious
mixture of old and new customs. As in olden
times, there are bonfires. But these are now
called St. John's Fire. And, of course, there is
a great deal of merrymaking.

In San Juan, Puerto Rico, bonfires blaze on
the beaches on St. John's Eve. Between
midnight and dawn, the people swim in the

sea, in memory of the saint who baptized people in the water. And Puerto Ricans in New York City take part in a gala San Juan Fiesta on the Sunday closest to June 24.

In Quebec, Canada, the *Fête de Saint-Jean-Baptiste*, also called *Fête Nationale des Québécois*, or Quebec National Day, is an important holiday. There are bonfires, fireworks, parades, and carnivals.

In New Mexico, American Indians celebrate the saint's birthday with corn dances. And throughout Mexico, fiestas fill the day Mexicans call *Dia de San Juan*.

Pueblo Indians in New Mexico celebrate the festival of Saint John the Baptist with a centuries-old corn dance.

July

1

Comte de Rochambeau (1725) French general who fought in the American Revolution

George Sand (1804) French writer

2

Sir Charles Tupper (1821) a prime minister of Canada

Thurgood Marshall (1908) first black justice of the U.S. Supreme Court

3

Alfred Korzybski (1879) Polish-born scientist and author

George M. Cohan (1878) American writer, actor, and musical composer

4

Calvin Coolidge (1872) 30th President of the United States

Louis Armstrong (1900) American jazz singer and trumpet player

Who shares my birthday?

Is your birthday in July? The names of some of the famous people born in July are shown on the calendar on this page and the next. What do you know about the person who shares your birthday?

5

David G. Farragut (1801) first admiral of the U.S. Navy

P. T. Barnum (1810) American showman who called his circus "The Greatest Show on Earth"

6

John Paul Jones (1747) American naval hero who is known as the "Father of the American Navy"

7

Gian Carlo Menotti (1911) American opera composer who wrote *Amahl and the Night Visitors*

Ringo Starr (1940) English drummer with the Beatles

8

Jean de la Fontaine (1621) French author of fables

Ferdinand von Zeppelin (1838) German inventor of airships

9

Elias Howe (1819) American inventor of the first practical sewing machine

Nikola Tesla (1856) electrical engineer, born in Austria-Hungary

10

Mary Bethune (1875) American educator

Arthur Ashe (1943) American tennis star

11

Robert Bruce (1274) Scottish king who freed Scotland from England

John Quincy Adams (1767) 6th President of the United States

12

Julius Caesar (100? B.C.) Roman military leader and statesman

Andrew Wyeth (1917) American artist; paints pictures of rural America

13

Mary Emma Woolley (1863) American educator who was president of Mount Holyoke College

14

James Abbott McNeil Whistler (1834) American painter

Gerald R. Ford (1913) 38th President of the United States

15

Rembrandt van Rijn (1606) Dutch painter

Maria Cabrini (1850) first U.S. citizen to be made a Roman Catholic saint

16

Mary Baker Eddy (1821) American founder of Christian Science

Roald Amundsen (1872) Norwegian explorer; discovered the South Pole

17

Isaac Watts (1674) English preacher and hymn writer

John Jacob Astor (1763) German-born fur trader

18

W. M. Thackeray (1811) English author who wrote *Vanity Fair*

John Glenn (1921) first American astronaut to orbit the earth

19

Samuel Colt (1814) American who developed a pistol named after him

Edgar Degas (1834) French painter

20

Petrarch (1304) Italian poet and scholar

Sir Edmund Hillary (1919) New Zealander; one of the first two men to reach the top of Mount Everest

21

Ernest Hemingway (1899) American author

Isaac Stern (1921) American violinist; debuted with the San Francisco Orchestra at age 11

22

Gregor Mendel (1822) Austrian botanist and monk who discovered rules of heredity

Stephen Vincent Benét (1898) American poet

23

Arthur W. Brown (1886) British aviator who made the first transatlantic flight

24

Simón Bolívar (1783) Venezuelan general who freed five nations

Amelia Earhart (1897) American; first woman to fly the Atlantic Ocean alone

25

Henry Knox (1750) American patriot; directed Washington's crossing of the Delaware River

Thomas Eakins (1844) American artist

26

George Bernard Shaw (1856) Irish-born playwright and critic

Carl Jung (1875) Swiss psychologist

27

Charlotte Corday (1768) French patriot

Leo Durocher (1906) American baseball player and manager of several baseball teams

28

Beatrix Potter (1866) British author and illustrator of *Peter Rabbit* and other children's books

29

Booth Tarkington (1869) American author of *Penrod* and other books

William Beebe (1877) American undersea explorer

30

Henry Ford (1863) American who founded Ford Motor Company

Casey Stengel (1890) American baseball player and manager

31

John Ericsson (1803) Swedish-American inventor

Evonne Goolagong Cawley (1951) Australian tennis player

The month of Julius Caesar

July is the seventh month of the year. It has thirty-one days. In ancient Roman times, when the year began in March, July was the fifth month of the year. It was called *Quintilis*, meaning "fifth."

When the Romans changed the calendar Quintilis became the seventh month. But it kept its original name. Much later, the Romans renamed this month *Julius*, in honor of Julius Caesar.

People living in England long ago had two names for this month. One name was *Maed-monath*, or "meadow month." For this was the month when farmers turned their cattle out to feed in the meadows.

This was also the time when farmers harvested hay to feed their cattle in winter. So the other name for this month was *Heg-monath*, or "hay month."

Until about two hundred years ago, people said JOO lee instead of ju LY. This is why, in some poems, July rhymes with such words as newly and truly.

The Police Pipe Band adds to the excitement of Canada Day in Vancouver, British Columbia.

Canada Day
July 1

Happy birthday, Canada!

Canada has a birthday on July 1. It's Canada Day, a national holiday that used to be called Dominion Day.

Canada once belonged to Great Britain. In time, parts of the country joined together to form their own government. This new nation, which remained loyal to Britain, was to be called the Dominion of Canada.

On July 1, 1867, the British government approved the plan. Canada became an independent country with its own government. The new Dominion of Canada had only four provinces. Now there are ten provinces and two territories.

Canada no longer calls itself a Dominion. It is just plain Canada, which is why Canadians now call July 1 Canada Day instead of Dominion Day.

Hands across the border

How would you like to go to a weeklong birthday party? That's just what Canadians in Windsor, Ontario, and Americans in Detroit, Michigan, do.

Canada's birthday, Canada Day, falls on July 1. And the birthday of the United States, Independence Day, falls on July 4. So, beginning on or just before July 1, the people of Windsor and Detroit join hands for a weeklong celebration that is called the International Freedom Festival.

Windsor is just across the Detroit River from Detroit. And it is on the river that the International Freedom Festival begins. Canadians and Americans line the shores as fireworks set off from big barges. After the fireworks, there are puppet shows, sky diving, water parades, and other events.

Happy birthday, America!

Red, white, and blue fireworks burst above the land from the Atlantic Ocean to the Pacific! It is July 4. On this day, the American people wish a happy birthday to their United States.

In the year 1607, English settlers landed at Jamestown, Virginia. In the following years, people from many countries came to America. Some came because they wanted a better life. Some wished to worship God in their own way. And almost all wanted land.

In a little more than a hundred years, there were thirteen English colonies in America. All were ruled by the king of England. As time went on, the Americans wanted a greater voice in their affairs. They wanted to make their own laws. They did not want a king to say how they should live. There was more and more trouble.

Finally, on April 19, 1775, there was a battle between American patriots and British soldiers. It was the beginning of the Revolutionary War. At first, the Americans simply fought to defend their rights. But before long, they wanted full independence.

On July 4, 1776, the American leaders approved the Declaration of Independence. This was an important paper. It said the people had the right to be free. The thirteen colonies united to fight for that freedom.

On the Fourth of July, fireworks burst over the Potomac River near Washington, D.C.

The war lasted eight years. Finally, in 1783, peace came. The people of this new land had won their freedom. On every Fourth of July, this fight for freedom is remembered all over America.

Independence Day, as the Fourth of July is also called, is a national holiday in the United States. Americans celebrate this day in all kinds of ways.

Girl Scouts, Boy Scouts, members of the armed forces, and schoolchildren take part in parades. Band members march by in bright uniforms. Americans take great pride in seeing the Stars and Stripes, their country's flag, held high to lead these parades.

It is a birthday salute to America. The Fourth of July is a celebration of freedom for people from many different countries.

Independence Day

by Laura Ingalls Wilder

In this story, taken from the book *Farmer Boy*, young Almanzo Wilder enjoys the Fourth of July as it was celebrated in northern New York more than a hundred years ago. Almanzo also learns how much fifty cents is really worth.

The Square was not really square. The railroad made it three-cornered. But everybody called it the Square, anyway. It was fenced, and grass grew there. Benches stood in rows on the grass, and people were filing between the benches and sitting down as they did in church.

Almanzo went with Father to one of the best front seats. All the important men stopped to shake hands with Father. The crowd kept coming till all the seats were full, and still there were people outside the fence.

The band stopped playing, and the minister prayed. Then the band tuned up again and everybody rose. Men and boys took off their hats. The band played, and everybody sang.

> Oh! say, can you see, by the dawn's early light,
> What so proudly we hailed at the twilight's last
>   gleaming?
> Whose broad stripes and bright stars, thro' the
>   perilous fight,
> O'er the ramparts we watched were so gallantly
>   streaming?

From the top of the flagpole, up against the blue sky, the Stars and Stripes were fluttering. Everybody looked at the American flag, and Almanzo sang with all his might.

Then everyone sat down, and a Congressman stood up on the platform. Slowly and solemnly he read the Declaration of Independence.

"When in the course of human events it becomes necessary for one people . . . to assume among the powers of the earth the separate and equal station. . . . We hold these truths to be self-evident, that all men are created equal. . . ."

Almanzo felt solemn and very proud.

Then two men made long political speeches. One believed in high tariffs, and one believed in free trade. All the grown-ups listened hard, but Almanzo did not understand the speeches very well and he began to be hungry. He was glad when the band played again.

The music was so gay; the bandsmen in their blue and red and their brass buttons tootled merrily, and the fat drummer beat rat-a-tat-tat on the drum. All the flags were fluttering and everybody was happy, because they were free

and independent and this was Independence
Day. And it was time to eat dinner.

Almanzo helped Father feed the horses while
Mother and the girls spread the picnic lunch
on the grass in the churchyard. Many others
were picnicking there, too, and after he had
eaten all he could Almanzo went back to the
Square.

There was a lemonade-stand by the hitching-
posts. A man sold pink lemonade, a nickel a
glass, and a crowd of the town boys were
standing around him. Cousin Frank was there.
Almanzo had a drink at the town pump, but
Frank said he was going to buy lemonade. He
had a nickel. He walked up to the stand and
bought a glass of the pink lemonade and drank
it slowly. He smacked his lips and rubbed his
stomach and said:

"Mmmm! Why don't you buy some?"

"Where'd you get the nickel?" Almanzo
asked. He had never had a nickel. Father gave
him a penny every Sunday to put in the
collection-box in church; he had never had any
other money.

"My father gave it to me," Frank bragged.
"My father gives me a nickel every time I ask
him."

"Well, so would my father if I asked him,"
said Almanzo.

"Well, why don't you ask him?" Frank did
not believe that Father would give Almanzo a
nickel. Almanzo did not know whether Father
would, or not.

"Because I don't want to," he said.

"He wouldn't give you a nickel," Frank said.

"He would, too."

"I dare you to ask him," Frank said. The other
boys were listening. Almanzo put his hands in
his pockets and said:

"I'd just as lief ask him if I wanted to."

"Yah, you're scared!" Frank jeered. "Double
dare! Double dare!"

Father was a little way down the street,

talking to Mr. Paddock, the wagon-maker. Almanzo walked slowly toward them. He was faint-hearted, but he had to go. The nearer he got to Father, the more he dreaded asking for a nickel. He had never before thought of doing such a thing. He was sure Father would not give it to him.

He waited till Father stopped talking and looked at him.

"What is it, son?" Father asked.

Almanzo was scared. "Father," he said.

"Well, son?"

"Father," Almanzo said, "would you—would you give me—a nickel?"

He stood there while Father and Mr. Paddock looked at him, and he wished he could get away. Finally Father asked:

"What for?"

Almanzo looked down at his moccasins and muttered:

"Frank had a nickel. He bought pink lemonade."

"Well," Father said, slowly, "if Frank treated you, it's only right you should treat him." Father put his hand in his pocket. Then he stopped and asked:

"Did Frank treat you to lemonade?"

Almanzo wanted so badly to get the nickel that he nodded. Then he squirmed and said:

"No, Father."

Father looked at him a long time. Then he took out his wallet and opened it, and slowly he took out a round, big silver half-dollar. He asked:

"Almanzo, do you know what this is?"

"Half a dollar," Almanzo answered.

"Yes. But do you know what half a dollar is?"

Almanzo didn't know it was anything but half a dollar.

"It's work, son," Father said. "That's what money is; it's hard work."

Mr. Paddock chuckled. "The boy's too young, Wilder," he said. "You can't make a youngster understand that."

"Almanzo's smarter than you think," said Father.

Almanzo didn't understand at all. He wished he could get away. But Mr. Paddock was looking at Father just as Frank looked at Almanzo when he double-dared him, and Father had said Almanzo was smart, so Almanzo tried to look like a smart boy. Father asked:

"You know how to raise potatoes, Almanzo?"

"Yes," Almanzo said.

"Say you have a seed potato in the spring, what do you do with it?"

"You cut it up," Almanzo said.

"Go on, son."

"Then you harrow—first you manure the field, and plow it. Then you harrow, and mark the ground. And plant the potatoes, and plow them, and hoe them. You plow and hoe them twice."

"That's right, son. And then?"

"Then you dig them and put them down cellar."

"Yes. Then you pick them over all winter;

221

you throw out all the little ones and the rotten ones. Come spring, you load them up and haul them here to Malone, and you sell them. And if you get a good price, son, how much do you get to show for all that work? How much do you get for half a bushel of potatoes?"

"Half a dollar," Almanzo said.

"Yes," said Father. "That's what's in this half-dollar, Almanzo. The work that raised half a bushel of potatoes is in it."

Almanzo looked at the round piece of money that Father held up. It looked small, compared with all that work.

"You can have it, Almanzo," Father said. Almanzo could hardly believe his ears. Father gave him the heavy half-dollar.

"It's yours," said Father. "You could buy a sucking pig with it, if you want to. You could raise it, and it would raise a litter of pigs, worth four, five dollars apiece. Or you can trade that half-dollar for lemonade, and drink it up. You do as you want, it's your money."

Almanzo forgot to say thank you. He held
the half-dollar a minute, then he put his hand
in his pocket and went back to the boys by the
lemonade-stand. The man was calling out,

"Step this way, step this way! Ice-cold
lemonade, pink lemonade, only five cents a
glass! Only half a dime, ice-cold pink lemonade!
The twentieth part of a dollar!"

Frank asked Almanzo:

"Where's the nickel?"

"He didn't give me a nickel," said Almanzo,
and Frank yelled:

"Yah, yah! I told you he wouldn't! I told you
so!"

"He gave me half a dollar," said Almanzo.

The boys wouldn't believe it till he showed
them. Then they crowded around, waiting for
him to spend it. He showed it to them all, and
put it back in his pocket.

"I'm going to look around," he said, "and buy
me a good little sucking pig."

The band came marching down the street,
and they all ran along beside it. The flag was
gloriously waving in front, then came the
buglers blowing and the fifers tootling and the
drummer rattling the drumsticks on the drum.
Up the street and down the street went the
band, with all the boys following it, and then
it stopped in the Square by the brass cannons.

Hundreds of people were there, crowding to
watch.

The cannons sat on their haunches, pointing
their long barrels upward. The band kept on
playing. Two men kept shouting, "Stand back!

Stand back!" and other men were pouring black powder into the cannons' muzzles and pushing it down with wads of cloth on long rods.

The iron rods had two handles, and two men pushed and pulled on them, driving the black powder down the brass barrels. Then all the boys ran to pull grass and weeds along the railroad tracks. They carried them by armfuls to the cannons, and the men crowded the weeds into the cannons' muzzles and drove them down with the long rods.

A bonfire was burning by the railroad tracks, and long iron rods were heating in it.

When all the weeds and grass had been packed tight against the powder in the cannons, a man took a little more powder in his hand

and carefully filled the two little touchholes in the barrels. Now everybody was shouting,

"Stand back! Stand back!"

Mother took hold of Almanzo's arm and made him come away with her. He told her:

"Aw, Mother, they're only loaded with powder and weeds. I won't get hurt, Mother. I'll be careful, honest." But she made him come away from the cannons.

Two men took the long iron rods from the fire. Everybody was still, watching. Standing as far behind the cannons as they could, the two men stretched out the rods and touched their red-hot tips to the touchholes. A little flame like a candle-flame flickered up from the powder. The little flames stood there burning; nobody breathed. Then—BOOM!

The cannons leaped backward, the air was full of flying grass and weeds. Almanzo ran with all the other boys to feel the warm muzzles of the cannons. Everybody was exclaiming about what a loud noise they had made.

"That's the noise that made the Redcoats run!" Mr. Paddock said to Father.

"Maybe," Father said, tugging his beard. "But it was muskets that won the Revolution. And don't forget it was axes and plows that made this country."

"That's so, come to think of it," Mr. Paddock said.

Independence Day was over. The cannons had been fired, and there was nothing more to do but hitch up the horses and drive home to do the chores.

If you enjoyed this story, you will want to read the rest of *Farmer Boy*, as well as all the other books in the "Little House" series.

Festival of Lanterns

People of almost all religions have special times for remembering their dead. Buddhists in Japan do this from July 13 to 15, on the festival of Bon.

Bon is also known as the Festival of Lanterns. This is the time of year when the spirits of the dead return to visit the living. Houses and graveyards are cleaned. And people buy food, incense, and decorations at special Bon markets.

At home, each family decorates a small altar. Food for the spirits is put on the altar. On the first evening, a lighted lantern is placed at the door to welcome the spirits. Then the family goes to the cemetery. There, they place food and lighted lanterns on the graves and invite the spirits to join them. The smell of incense fills the air.

During the next two days, while the spirits are visiting, families may entertain guests. And people often exchange gifts. On the last day, rice balls are put out for the spirits to eat on their return journey.

That night, families living near the water gather for a final farewell to the spirits. Small paper lanterns are lit and set on little wooden floats. Then the people place the floats in the water and watch them slowly drift away into the dark. The spirits are on their way back to the other world.

On the last day of the Festival of Lanterns,
Buddhists in Japan set lighted lanterns adrift
on the water. The little lantern boats carry the
spirits of the dead back to the spirit world.

A bit of Scotland

Highland games are contests in athletics, dancing, and music. Events of this kind were first held in the rugged Highlands of northern Scotland. Today, you can see these games all over the United States, in Canada, and in some other countries.

The largest and most popular festival of this kind in the United States is held on the second weekend in July. It takes place at Grandfather Mountain, near Linville, North Carolina, and is called Highland Games and Gathering of Scottish Clans.

A clan is a large group of related families with the same last name. You can tell one Scottish clan from another by their tartan—the plaid design on their clothes.

Each year, a hundred or more clans gather at Grandfather Mountain. There are all kinds of track and field events—foot races, high jumping, broad jumping—even a tug-of-war.

Meanwhile, men and women in colorful kilts (pleated skirts) perform the sword dance, the Scottish Reel, and the Highland Fling. And the mountains echo with the wail of bagpipes and the thunder of drums.

There are also contests of strength, such as tossing the caber. A caber looks like a short telephone pole. It may be 20 feet (6 meters) long and weigh as much as 150 pounds (68 kilograms).

Tossing the caber takes a lot of strength.

Scottish dancing is one of the many contests held at all Highland Games.

The contestant picks the caber up by the narrow end. Holding it upright, he staggers off to a running start. Then he tosses the caber so that it falls end over end.

But the best comes on Sunday afternoon. First, the Massed Bands pass in review. Then, banners blowing in the breeze, comes the Parade of Tartans.

Long live France!

Bastille Day
July 14

This French family is putting up colorful pennants in preparation for Bastille Day.

In France, July 14 means much the same as July 4 does in the United States. It's a national holiday, when everyone celebrates the country's independence. The French call this holiday Bastille Day, or *Fête Nationale.*

In Paris, France, on July 14, 1789, a ragged mob swept through the streets shouting for justice. The men and women were on their way to the Bastille, a prison that once was a fort.

The Bastille stood for all that was evil in France. Under the king, the rich paid no taxes on land and lived in luxury. The poor were heavily taxed, and often hungry and starving. If anyone spoke up about the unfairness, that person was thrown into the Bastille and forgotten.

But on that memorable day in July, the mob rose up in anger. They stormed the Bastille, killed the guards, and freed the prisoners. The next day they began to tear down the hated prison, stone by stone.

It was the beginning of the French Revolution. The people of France wanted their freedom, and the chance to be treated as equals.

The joyful celebration of Bastille Day begins the night before with a torchlight parade. At daybreak, cannons announce the arrival of the new day. There are parades, games, speeches, and shows.

At night, public buildings and fountains are lighted. Fireworks burst in the sky. And the people dance in the streets until dawn, just as they did long ago on the first Bastille Day.

The Bastille Day parade in Paris is an exciting event. The huge memorial in the distance is the Arc de Triomphe. France's Unknown Soldier of World War I is buried there.

The Liberator

Simón Bolívar is one of the greatest heroes of South America. Known as *El Libertador* (The Liberator), Bolívar is also called the "George Washington of South America."

Bolívar, like Washington, was a great general. He fought for the freedom of the Spanish colonies in South America.

Washington became the first President of the United States. And in 1819, Bolívar became the first president of a union of South American countries. Finally, in 1824, Bolívar crushed the Spanish army. He had won independence for Bolivia, Colombia, Ecuador, Peru, and Venezuela.

Simón Bolívar's birthday, July 24, is especially remembered in the city of Caracas, Venezuela, where he was born and is buried. The country of Bolivia was named in his honor, and a silver coin used today in Venezuela is called the bolívar.

Island holiday

Christopher Columbus landed in what is now Puerto Rico in 1493. It was his second voyage to the New World. He claimed the beautiful island for Spain. The name Puerto Rico is Spanish for "Rich Port."

For more than four hundred years, Puerto Ricans lived under Spanish rule. But after the Spanish-American War in 1898, Spain gave up Puerto Rico to the United States.

Puerto Rico adopted its own constitution on July 25, 1952. On that day, Puerto Rico became a free commonwealth with its own governor. This means it's protected and helped by the United States.

Puerto Ricans are American citizens. They can move to the mainland if they wish. But those living on the island cannot vote in presidential elections.

On July 25, there are parades, speeches, speedboat races, and all kinds of fireworks. Constitution Day is Puerto Rico's most important holiday.

August

1

Francis Scott Key
(1779) American who
wrote "The Star-
Spangled Banner"

Maria Mitchell
(1818) American
astronomer and Hall
of Fame member

2

John Tyndall (1820)
British physicist

Moses Coit Tyler
(1835) American
author and first
professor of
American history in
the United States

3

Ernie Pyle (1900)
American journalist
of World War II
fame; won a Pulitzer
Prize in 1944 for his
newspaper columns
about American
soldiers in action

4

**Percy Bysshe
Shelley** (1792)
English poet

Knut Hamsun
(1859) Norwegian
author and 1920
Nobel Prize winner
for literature

Who shares
my birthday?

Is your birthday in August? The names of
some of the famous people born in August
are shown on the calendar on this page and
the next. What do you know about the
person who shares your birthday?

5

Ruth Sawyer (1880)
American author of
children's books

Neil Armstrong
(1930) American
astronaut; first
person to set foot on
the moon

6

**Alfred, Lord
Tennyson** (1809)
English poet

**Sir Alexander
Fleming** (1881)
British scientist who
discovered penicillin

7

Louis Leakey (1903)
British scientist who
found evidence of
human origins

Ralph Bunche
(1904) American
statesman; won the
Nobel Peace Prize

8

Sara Teasdale
(1884) American poet

**Marjorie Kinnan
Rawlings** (1896)
American author of
The Yearling and
other stories about
children and animals

9

Izaak Walton (1593)
English author of
*The Compleat
Angler*, a classic
book on fishing

John Dryden (1631)
English poet and
playwright

10

Herbert Hoover
(1874) 31st President
of the United States

Jimmy Dean (1928)
American country
and western singer

11

**Carrie Jacobs
Bond** (1862)
American writer of
popular songs

Alex Haley (1921)
American author; his
book *Roots* was
adapted for TV

12

**Katharine Lee
Bates** (1859)
American poet who
wrote the words to
the hymn "America
the Beautiful"

13

Lucy Stone (1818)
American women's
rights leader

Annie Oakley
(1860) American who
was famous for her
accurate shooting

14

John Galsworthy
(1867) English author

**John Ringling
North** (1903)
American whose
family ran the
world's largest circus

15

**Napoleon
Bonaparte** (1769)
military genius and
emperor of France

Sir Walter Scott
(1771) Scottish
author of *Ivanhoe*

16

Gabriel Lippmann
(1845) French
physicist and Nobel
Prize winner

Fess Parker (1927)
American actor who
played Davy
Crockett

17

Davy Crockett
(1786) American
frontiersman who
was killed defending
the Alamo

18

Virginia Dare
(1587) first English
child born in America

Roberto Clemente
(1934) Puerto Rican
baseball player who
won fame as a hitter

19

Orville Wright
(1871) pioneer
American aviator and
airplane designer

Willie Shoemaker
(1931) American
jockey

20

**Oliver Hazard
Perry** (1785)
American naval
officer; hero of the
Battle of Lake Erie

Benjamin Harrison
(1833) 23rd President
of the United States

21

Count Basie (1904)
American jazz pianist

Wilt Chamberlain
(1936) American
basketball star

22

Claude Debussy
(1862) French
composer

Dorothy Parker
(1893) American
author

23

Baron Cuvier
(1769) French
naturalist who began
the study of fossils

Edgar Lee Masters
(1869) American poet
and biographer

24

George Stubbs
(1724) English animal
painter

Shirley Hufstedler
(1925) American
jurist; first U.S.
secretary of
education

25

Bret Harte (1836)
American author of
colorful stories about
the West

Althea Gibson
(1927) American
tennis player

26

Antoine Lavoisier
(1743) French
chemist

Lee De Forest
(1873) American
inventor and radio
pioneer

27

Margaretha Schurz
(1833) German-born
educator who
established the first
U.S. kindergarten

Lyndon B. Johnson
(1908) 36th President
of the U.S.

28

**Johann von
Goethe** (1749)
German writer

**Elizabeth Ann
Seton** (1774) first
American-born
Catholic saint

29

**Oliver Wendell
Holmes** (1809)
American author and
doctor

Maurice Maeterlinck
(1862) Belgian poet
and playwright

30

Mary Shelley (1797)
English author of
Frankenstein

Ernest Rutherford
(1871) British
physicist; "father of
nuclear science"

31

Maria Montessori
(1870) Italian
educator

Wilhelmina (1880)
queen of the
Netherlands

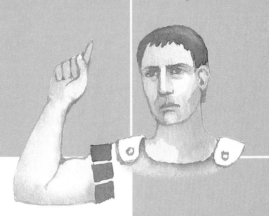

The month of Augustus

August is the eighth month of the year. It has thirty-one days. In ancient Roman times, when the year began in March, August was the sixth month and had thirty days. This month was called *Sextilis*, meaning "sixth."

After Julius Caesar was killed, Augustus, his nephew, became emperor of Rome. The Romans wanted to honor Augustus by naming a month for him, just as they had done for his uncle. Augustus chose to have the month Sextilis renamed in his honor.

Long ago, the English people had many names for August. One was *Weod-monath*, or "Weed month." During this month, weeds grew rapidly. Another name was *Scere-monath*, or "Shear month," because sheep had their wool sheared, or cut off, at this time.

Since August was also the month when the first wheat was harvested, a feast was held to give thanks for the grain used to make loaves of bread. This custom gave the month the name *Hlaf-maesse*, or "Loaf Feast."

237

**Mountain Dance
and Folk Festival**

Along about sundown

Thrill to the music of the banjos, fiddles, and dulcimers. And listen as the caller sings out the steps for the square dance:

"Wave the ocean, wave the sea,
Wave that pretty girl back to me!"

You're at the yearly Mountain Dance and Folk Festival in Asheville, North Carolina. This festival starts "along about sundown" on the first Thursday in August and lasts through Saturday. It's a time when people

from Hominy Valley, Hanging Dog, Turkey
Creek, and other towns in the Great Smokies
and Blue Ridge Mountains get together to
sing and dance to their special music.

You'll hear such songs as "Sourwood
Mountain," "Soldier's Joy," and "Pretty
Polly." There is music and dancing the way
these mountain people have done it for
hundreds of years.

From all over the country, and from parts
of Europe, young and old alike come to enjoy
the oldest dance and folk festival in America.
So pick your partner and join in:

"Swing her high, swing her low,
Don't step on that pretty little toe!"

Tanabata Matsuri

The princess and the cowherd

Once upon a time, two stars, Vega and Altair, fell in love. Vega was a princess, the daughter of the king of the heavens. Altair was a cowherd. Even so, the king allowed them to marry.

Vega was so happy, she no longer did her weaving. And Altair was so in love he let the cows wander away. This made the king angry. He sent Altair to live on the far side of the Milky Way—the Heavenly River. And

he ruled that the two lovers might see each other only once a year—on the seventh day of the seventh moon.

When this day came, Vega could not find a way to cross the Milky Way. She began to weep bitter tears. A flock of magpies saw how sad she was and took pity on her. The magpies spread their wings to make a bridge across the Heavenly River. Vega ran lightly over their wings and into the arms of the waiting Altair.

Ever since, according to this ancient Chinese fairy tale, this is the way Vega and Altair have met. But if it rains on this day, the magpies cannot make a bridge. Then, Vega and Altair must wait another year.

The Japanese have long loved this story. They call the day *Tanabata Matsuri* or "Weaving-Loom Festival." It is also known as the *Hoshi* or "Star Festival."

In most of Japan, *Tanabata* is celebrated on July 7. But one city, Sendai, joyously celebrates *Tanabata Matsuri* on August 7.

In Sendai, long bamboo poles are set up so that they lean out over the streets. Colorful paper chains and streamers are fastened to the poles. And bamboo branches are placed in front of houses or in gardens. The children decorate the branches with colored figures made of paper.

The day after *Tanabata*, these bamboo branches are put into the nearest stream. They are then allowed to float away. Doing this brings good luck.

Father of India

In India, a wise and holy person is called a mahatma (muh HAHT muh). The title means "great soul." The greatest mahatma of all was Mohandas Karamchand Gandhi. He is known as the "father of India."

As a leader, Gandhi was against violence. He believed that how a person behaves is more important than what one succeeds in doing. He won many followers.

Gandhi worked many years for India's freedom from Great Britain. The day he dreamed of finally came on August 15, 1947. But it was also a sad day. Quarrels between Hindus and Muslims had caused many riots. Because of religious differences, Gandhi's beloved India was divided into two countries—India and Pakistan.

Gandhi, a Hindu, believed that people of all religions could live together in peace. But this was not to be. On January 30, 1948, Gandhi was shot to death by a man who feared what the Mahatma believed.

Mahatma Gandhi led his country to freedom.

Indonesian holiday

A *betjak* (BEH chahk) is a kind of taxi for one or two passengers. It looks like a bicycle with three wheels. The driver pedals from the rear.

You can see many *betjaks* in Jakarta, the capital city of Indonesia. Jakarta is on the island of Java, in Southeast Asia. Java is only one of more than thirteen thousand islands that make up the nation of Indonesia.

For many years, the Dutch ruled most of the islands of Indonesia. But on August 17, 1945, Indonesia declared its independence. This was also the day the red and white flag became the official flag of the country.

In the city of Jakarta, flags fly everywhere on Independence Day—even on *betjaks*. As the drivers pedal through the busy streets, clanging their bells as they go, the red and white flag of Indonesia flaps in the breeze.

A shining salute

Every year, in August, the city of St. Augustine, Florida, has a birthday party that lasts for four days. It is called "Days in Spain," because the city was settled by people from Spain.

In 1565, the king of Spain sent Don Pedro Menéndez de Avilés to Florida to drive out the French. Menéndez first saw the shore of the future city on August 28, the feast day of Saint Augustine. After sailing north to check on the French, Menéndez returned to St. Augustine.

On September 8, 1565, with banners waving, trumpets sounding, and cannons booming, Menéndez claimed the land for Spain. He named the new settlement for Saint Augustine.

The official birthday of the city is on September 8. But the big celebration—Days in Spain—comes earlier, around the middle of August. This makes it possible for more people to come to the party. At this time of year, children are still out of school. So, they can ride ponies, play games, and watch puppet plays while their parents also enjoy the fiesta.

Musicians stroll along St. George Street, playing Spanish songs on guitars and accordians. Castanets click as dancers do the flamenco, a Spanish Gypsy dance in which there is much hand clapping and a great deal of foot-stamping. And, of course, Spanish food is served.

On the last night of the fiesta, the candles on a huge birthday cake are lighted. This birthday cake now has more than four hundred candles—one for each year since 1565. The cake is a shining salute to St. Augustine, Florida, the oldest city in the United States.

Spanish soldiers, dressed in breastplates and helmets, fight the French for control of Florida. Actors present this show as part of the "Days in Spain" celebration in St. Augustine, Florida.

September

1

Edgar Rice Burroughs (1875) American author of "Tarzan" novels

Rocky Marciano (1923) heavyweight boxing champion

2

Lydia Kamekeha Liliuokalani (1838) queen of Hawaii

Eugene Field (1850) American writer, often called "The Poet of Childhood"

3

Sarah Orne Jewett (1849) American author of stories about New England

Macfarlane Burnet (1899) Australian doctor and expert in virus diseases

4

François-René de Chateaubriand (1768) French author

Richard Wright (1908) American author

Who shares my birthday?

Is your birthday in September? The names of some of the famous people born in September are shown on the calendar on this page and the next. What do you know about the person who shares your birthday?

5

Johann Christian Bach (1735) German composer and organist

Jesse James (1847) a colorful character of the Old West

6

Marquis de Lafayette (1757) French soldier and statesman

Jane Addams (1860) American social reformer

7

Elizabeth I (1533) queen of England

Grandma Moses (1860) American painter whose full name was Anna Mary Robertson Moses

8

Antonín Dvořák (1841) Czech composer

Robert A. Taft (1889) U.S. senator from Ohio

9

Cardinal Richelieu (1585) French statesman

Harland Sanders (1890) Colonel Sanders of Kentucky Fried Chicken fame

10

Arnold Palmer (1929) American golf champion

Jose Feliciano (1945) American composer and guitarist

11

William Porter (1862) American author who wrote under the name of O. Henry

James H. Jeans (1877) English scientist

12

Irène Joliot-Curie (1897) French scientist and Nobel Prize winner

Jesse Owens (1913) American athlete and Olympic champion

13

Walter Reed (1851) American doctor who proved mosquitoes carry yellow fever

John J. Pershing (1860) U.S. general in World War I

14

Alexander von Humboldt (1769) German scientist and geographer

Margaret Sanger (1883) founder of Planned Parenthood

15

James Fenimore Cooper (1789) American; wrote *The Last of the Mohicans*

William H. Taft (1857) 27th President of the United States

16

Francis Parkman (1823) American historian and writer

James J. Hill (1838) American railroad builder, known as the "Empire Builder"

17

Friedrich Augustin von Steuben (1730) German who fought in American Revolution

Hank Williams (1923) writer and singer of country and western songs

18

Samuel Johnson (1709) English author who is famous for writing a dictionary

John Diefenbaker (1895) a prime minister of Canada

19

Lajos Kossuth (1802) Hungarian patriot

Rachel Field (1894) American author of *Hitty, Her First Hundred Years,* and other children's books

20

Elizabeth Kenny (1886) Australian nurse who helped victims of polio

Jelly Roll Morton (1885) composer of American ragtime and jazz music

21

Girolamo Savonarola (1452) Italian religious reformer

Louis Jolliet (1645) French-Canadian explorer

22

Lord Chesterfield (1694) English statesman and author

Michael Faraday (1791) English scientist

23

William McGuffey (1800) American educator; published the McGuffey readers

Louise Nevelson (1900) American sculptress

24

F. Scott Fitzgerald (1895) American novelist and short-story writer

James Henson (1936) American puppeteer, creator of the "Muppets"

25

William H. Hughes (1862) prime minister of Australia

Barbara Walters (1931) American newscaster and interviewer

26

Johnny Appleseed (1774) American pioneer planter of apple trees; real name John Chapman

George Gershwin (1898) American composer

27

Samuel Adams (1722) American patriot

Thomas Nast (1840) American cartoonist; started present-day idea of Santa Claus

28

Frances E. Willard (1839) American educator

Kate Douglas Wiggin (1856) American author of children's books

29

Horatio Nelson (1758) Britain's greatest admiral and naval hero

Enrico Fermi (1901) Italian-American nuclear physicist

30

Hans Wilhelm Geiger (1882) German inventor of the Geiger counter

Truman Capote (1924) American author

The "seventh" month

September is the ninth month of the year. It has thirty days. In ancient Roman times, when the year began in March, September was the seventh month. The Roman name *September* comes from *septem,* the Latin word for "seven."

When the Romans made January the first month, September became the ninth month of the year. But the Romans did not bother to change its name. Later, several Roman emperors tried to rename September, but with no success.

Long ago, in England, this month had two names. One was *Haervest-monath,* or "Harvest month." The main crop at this time of year was barley. So this month was also called *Gerst-monath,* which means "barley month."

A "take it easy" day

It's Labor Day! Let's have a picnic! Let's go to a ball game! Or, let's just take it easy!

In the United States, Canada, and Puerto Rico, Labor Day is a national holiday. It is celebrated on the first Monday in September. Because of this, Labor Day has become a symbol of the end of the summer.

The idea for Labor Day probably came from a carpenter named Peter McGuire. At a labor union meeting McGuire suggested that a special day be set aside to honor working people. This new holiday was first observed in New York City on September 5, 1882.

Many countries celebrate a special day for working people. In New Zealand, this day is called Labour Day. It is celebrated on the fourth Monday in October. In Australia, the date of Labour Day, also called Eight-Hour Day, varies from state to state. And in Europe, many countries celebrate Labor Day on May 1 (see pages 166-167).

Labor Day is often a time for parades, picnics, and special events. But many working people like to use their special day as a time for "taking it easy."

Honoring Native Americans

Tom-toms thump and rattles clatter as brightly clad dancers stamp and shuffle. Strange chants fill the air. There's a roar of applause as a skillful rider manages to stay on a wildly bucking horse. Movement, color, and excitement are everywhere. This is the Navajo Nation Fair, held the second week of September at Window Rock, Arizona.

The Navajo (NAV uh hoh) nation is the largest Indian tribe in the United States. About a hundred thousand Navajo live on a huge reservation that covers parts of Arizona, Utah, and New Mexico. There are also thousands of other Navajo who live in cities and towns.

A great number of the Navajo are farmers or sheep ranchers, but many others work in businesses and industries that are owned by the tribe. Although the Navajo have kept many of their old customs, they also make use of modern ways.

The Navajo Nation Fair is the largest Native American Fair in the United States. It is held to show off the arts and crafts of Indians, as well as to honor and remember the old ways of life. Indians of many tribes other than the Navajo take part in the fair.

Visitors to the fair can see old ceremonies and dances, and listen to ancient songs and music. They can eat traditional Navajo foods.

Barrel racing is one of many exciting events at the Navajo Nation Fair.

And they can see how Indians of long ago made things and did things.

There are also many "modern" events to see, such as a horse race, a rodeo, and a Miss Navajo contest.

Native Americans are also honored in other parts of the United States on the fourth Friday of September. This day is American Indian Day in Arizona, California, Connecticut, and Illinois. An American Indian Day is also observed in a number of other states in other months.

A special event much like the Navajo Nation Fair is held in Anadarko, Oklahoma, in August. It is the American Indian Exposition, put on by twelve of the Plains tribes. There,

Indians dressed in their tribal costumes stage a great parade. This is followed by dances, games, and other events. The Exposition lasts five days.

People from some thirty North American tribes also get together at the All American Indian Days at Sheridan, Wyoming. At this event, which takes place at the end of July or the first part of August, there are Indian dances, ceremonies, and many other interesting things to see.

Throughout the year there are many smaller Indian festivals and celebrations in the United States and Canada. All of these are put on by Native Americans to honor their past and their present ways of life.

Indian children, dressed in costumes, take part in a harvest celebration in New Mexico.

Gifts for ghosts

Have you ever heard of ghost money, orphan ghosts, or hungry ghosts? All these things are part of a holiday called the Feast of the Hungry Ghosts, which is celebrated in Singapore.

Singapore is a small island country in Asia. About three-fourths of the people of Singapore are Chinese. The Feast of the Hungry Ghosts is one of their special holidays. Other people of Singapore do not celebrate the feast.

The Singapore Chinese believe that the souls of the dead roam the earth during the month of September. On a special day, people offer gifts to the spirits of their ancestors. They also do this for "orphan" ghosts who have no one to care for them.

The gifts are mostly food, clothes, and pretend paper money called "ghost money." It is believed that if these things are burnt up, the spirits will get them. They will then have food to eat, clothes to wear, and money to spend.

"Independence or death!"

In the year 1822, a handsome young man stood on a riverbank in Brazil. He was Dom Pedro Bragansa, son of the king of Portugal and the leader of the Brazilian people.

For hundreds of years, Portugal had ruled Brazil. Now, the government of Portugal had passed harsh new laws that would take away much of Brazil's freedom. Brazil had sent men to plead for a change in the laws.

Dom Pedro's face grew grim as he read messages that had just come from Portugal. The messages said that the government of Portugal would not listen. The Brazilian leaders had been ordered to Portugal to go on trial for treason!

Dom Pedro threw down the messages. He snatched off his hat and waved it in the air. In a loud voice he shouted, "Independence or death!"

Less than two years later, Brazil had won its independence and was a free country. September 7, the day when Dom Pedro gave his defiant shout, is now celebrated as Brazil's Independence Day.

Jewish New Year

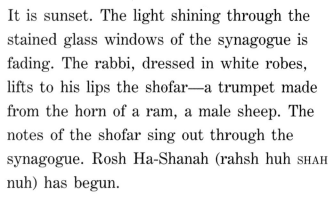

It is sunset. The light shining through the stained glass windows of the synagogue is fading. The rabbi, dressed in white robes, lifts to his lips the shofar—a trumpet made from the horn of a ram, a male sheep. The notes of the shofar sing out through the synagogue. Rosh Ha-Shanah (rahsh huh SHAH nuh) has begun.

Rosh Ha-Shanah (or Rosh Hashanah) means "beginning of the year." It is the Jewish New Year celebration. For Jewish people, this is a very important religious holiday. It is known as the Day of Judgment, or the Day of Remembrance.

At this time, God writes in the Book of Life what is to happen to every person. But prayer and sorrow for one's sins can change what is written before the Book of Life is closed on Yom Kippur (see page 258). So, during the next ten days, Jews pray and express their sorrow for any wrongs they have done during the year just ended.

Some Jews celebrate Rosh Ha-Shanah for only one day, from sunset to sunset. Others celebrate for two days. During this time, people go to special services at a synagogue. On the afternoon of the first day, many people take part in a special ceremony. They go to a river or lake, where they pray to have their sins carried away by the water.

In the evening, people light candles in their

homes and sit down to a holiday meal. Some
of the food is special holiday food. There are
round, smooth loaves of bread that stand for
a smooth, happy year to come. And there are
apples dipped in honey. These stand for a
"sweet" year, with no sadness in it.

In the Jewish calendar (see page 27), Rosh
Ha-Shanah falls on the first day of the month
of Tishri. It can come anywhere between
September 5 and October 5.

An apple and honey treat

Would you like to enjoy a
Jewish New Year treat?
All you need is an apple
and a small bowl of honey.

Ask a grown-up to cut
an apple into slices. If you
sprinkle lemon juice on the
slices, it will keep them
from turning brown.

Arrange the apple slices
around a bowl of honey
and your treat is ready.

Dip a slice of apple into
the honey and eat.
Mmmmm!

Yom Kippur

The Day of Atonement

In the Hebrew language, *Yom Kippur* (YAHM KIHP uhr or YOHM KIH poor) means "Day of Atonement." Atonement means to make up for something bad you have done. For Jewish people, Yom Kippur is a day when they try to think of all the wrongs they have done and ask God's forgiveness.

Yom Kippur is the most important and holiest day of the Jewish year. It comes nine

days after Rosh Ha-Shanah (see page 256).
Like all Jewish holy days, Yom Kippur begins
at sunset. Most people go to a service at a
synagogue in the evening and again the
following morning.

From the beginning of Yom Kippur until
sunset the next day, people do not eat or
drink anything—not even water. The day is
spent quietly at home. In the late afternoon,
many people go to another synagogue service.
At sunset, a blast on the shofar, or ram's
horn, is a sign that God has closed the Book
of Life. The Day of Atonement is over.

The Cry of Dolores

Grimly, Father Hidalgo, priest of the little Mexican community of Dolores, tugged at the rope that rang the church bell. He was calling the people to church earlier than usual on this Sunday morning.

It was September 15, 1810, and on this day, Father Hidalgo was going to give a very different kind of sermon. He was going to call on the Mexican people to rise up and free themselves from Spain.

The speech Father Hidalgo gave that morning became known as *Grito de Dolores*, or "Cry of Dolores." It was the beginning of years of war. Father Hidalgo, who is often called the "Father of Mexican Independence," didn't live to see an independent Mexico. He was killed in 1811, but Mexico won its independence in 1821.

September 16, the day after Father Hidalgo gave the Cry of Dolores, is celebrated as Mexico's Independence Day. On the eve of Independence Day, the president of Mexico repeats the Cry of Dolores. Then he rings the same church bell that Father Hidalgo rang. Bells throughout Mexico ring out in honor of a free Mexico.

The drill master

At the beginning of the American
Revolutionary War, most men in the
American Army were farmers and working
men. They were brave, but they had no
experience as soldiers. They didn't know how
to march properly, how to obey commands, or
how to load and shoot as fast as the
experienced enemy soldiers. This caused them
to lose some battles.

In 1777, a Prussian army officer, Baron
Friedrich von Steuben, came to America.
Steuben knew all the things a soldier has to
know and how to teach these things.

General George Washington sent Steuben
to Valley Forge to drill, or train, the
American army. Steuben worked all winter.
By spring, he had the Americans trained.
Truly, he had earned the nickname "Drill
Master of the American Revolution."

Steuben was made a Major General and
fought in a number of battles. After the war,
he became an American citizen. His birthday,
September 17, is celebrated with parades in
some cities.

Autumn's Eve

In Korea, autumn is a long and pleasant season. The weather is usually nice, and the grain and fruit are ripe and ready to eat. Farmers have gathered in most of the crops. Their long, hard summer of work is over.

So, for the people of Korea, the beginning of autumn is a time of thanksgiving. They celebrate it with a day called Ch'usok, which means "Autumn's Eve." This day, also known as the Moon Festival, falls on the fifteenth day of the eighth lunar month, usually near the end of September.

Ch'usok is a happy day. People visit the tombs of their ancestors to pay their respects at this happy time. They also leave gifts of food for the dead.

There are parties, with games and dancing. Some people exchange gifts. On the eve of Ch'usok, many Koreans have a special "moon cake," made with rice, chestnuts, and fruit.

Korean-Americans perform a farmer's dance during the Ch'usok festival in New York City.

Oktoberfest

Eat, drink, and be merry!

Teams of big horses, decorated with gay, colorful ribbons, clip-clop through the streets. They are pulling huge wagons loaded with barrels of beer. The oompah, toot, and thump of brass bands fills the air. There are banners, decorations, bright costumes and merriment everywhere. It's the Oktoberfest, or October Festival, in the city of Munich, Germany!

Although it is called the Oktoberfest, this sixteen-day celebration begins in September. It comes to an end on the first Sunday in October. The first Oktoberfest was held in 1810, to celebrate the wedding of King Ludwig and his queen, Theresa. But today, the Oktoberfest is really just an excuse for people to have fun!

This team of powerful workhorses is pulling a wagon loaded with beer barrels. It is all part of the Oktoberfest parade held each year in Munich, Germany.

At the beginning of Oktoberfest, there's a big parade of bands and floats. The marchers come from all parts of Germany, and from many other countries as well. In a big park near the center of the city, there are merry-go-rounds and side shows. And there are decorated booths at which people can buy all sorts of things. There are also huge tents in which thousands of people at a time can eat and drink.

And eating and drinking are an important part of Oktoberfest! At the park, people can feast on all kinds of sausages, cheeses, fried fish on sticks, fried and roasted chicken—even whole roasted oxen. Of course, the main Oktoberfest drink is beer, for the city of Munich is famous for its beer.

Each year, millions of people from all over the world come to Munich just for the Oktoberfest. It's one of the world's happiest holiday events!

October

1

James Lawrence
(1781) American
naval officer in the
War of 1812

Jimmy Carter
(1924) 39th President
of the United States

2

Mohandas K. Gandhi (1869)
Indian political
leader, known as the
"Father of India"

Cordell Hull (1871)
American statesman

3

George Bancroft
(1800) American
historian, teacher,
and diplomat

Eleonora Duse
(1859) Italian actress,
called "greatest of
her time"

4

Rutherford B. Hayes
(1822) 19th President
of the United States

Frederic Remington (1861)
American artist;
known for paintings of
the American West

Who shares my birthday?

Is your birthday in October? The names of
some of the famous people born in October
are shown on the calendar on this page and
the next. What do you know about the
person who shares your birthday?

5

Chester A. Arthur
(1829) 21st President
of the United States

Pablo Picasso
(1881) Spanish artist;
founder of cubist
school

6

Jenny Lind (1820)
singer known as the
"Swedish Nightingale"

Thor Heyerdahl
(1914) Norwegian
explorer

7

James Whitcomb Riley (1849)
American known as
the "Hoosier Poet"

Niels Bohr (1885)
Danish physicist who
won the 1922 Nobel
Prize for physics

8

Eddie Rickenbacker
(1890) American ace
in World War I

Jesse Jackson
(1941) American
minister and civil
rights leader

9

Camille Saint-Saëns (1835)
French composer

Giuseppe Verdi
(1813) Italian opera
composer

10

Fridtjof Nansen
(1861) Norwegian
explorer and
statesman

Helen Hayes (1900)
American actress,
known as the "First
Lady of the Theater"

11

Eleanor Roosevelt
(1884) American
humanitarian and wife
of President Franklin
D. Roosevelt

Jerome Robbins
(1918) American
ballet dancer

12

Ralph Vaughan Williams (1872)
British composer

Dick Gregory
(1932) American
comedian, author,
and political activist

13

Arna Bontemps
(1902) American
author of *Story of
the Negro*

Margaret Thatcher
(1925) British prime
minister

14

Dwight D. Eisenhower (1890)
34th President of the
United States

Lois Lenski (1893)
American author and
illustrator

15

Virgil (70 B.C.)
greatest poet of
ancient Rome

Helen Hunt Jackson (1830)
American author of
Ramona

16

Noah Webster (1758) American educator who compiled *Webster's Dictionary*

Oscar Wilde (1854) Irish author, noted for his wit

17

Jimmy Breslin (1930) American journalist

William Anders (1933) American astronaut and ambassador to Norway

18

Henri Bergson (1859) French philosopher and 1927 Nobel Prize winner for literature

Pierre E. Trudeau (1919) a prime minister of Canada

19

John McLoughlin (1784) Canadian pioneer, known as the "Father of Oregon"

20

Sir Christopher Wren (1632) English architect

Mickey Mantle (1931) New York Yankee baseball star from 1951 to 1968

21

Hokusai (1760) Japanese artist

Alfred Nobel (1833) Swedish chemist who invented dynamite and founded Nobel Prizes

22

Franz Liszt (1811) Hungarian composer and most celebrated pianist of his time

23

Gertrude Ederle (1907?) American who was the first woman to swim the English Channel

Pelé (1941) Brazilian soccer star

24

Anton van Leeuwenhoek (1632) Dutch scientist

Sarah Josepha Hale (1788) American editor who wrote "Mary Had a Little Lamb"

25

Johann Strauss, Jr. (1825) Austrian composer known as the "Waltz King"

Richard Byrd (1888) American admiral and explorer of the Arctic and Antarctic

26

Mahalia Jackson (1911) American gospel singer

Shah Mohammad Reza Pahlavi (1919) last shah of Iran

27

James Cook (1728) British navigator and explorer of the Pacific Ocean

Theodore Roosevelt (1858) 26th President of the United States

28

Jonas Salk (1914) American research scientist; developed a vaccine to fight polio

Bruce Jenner (1949) American Olympic decathlon winner

29

James Boswell (1740) Scottish author of *The Life of Samuel Johnson*

Jean Giraudoux (1882) French playwright

30

John Adams (1735) 2nd President of the United States

Richard Sheridan (1751) Irish playwright

31

Juliette Low (1860) founder of the Girl Scouts of America

Dan Rather (1931) American television broadcast journalist

The "eighth" month

October is the tenth month of the year. It has thirty-one days. In ancient Roman times, when the year began in March, October was the eighth month of the year. This month got its name from *octo*, the Latin word for "eight."

When the Romans made January the first month of the year, October became the tenth month. The Roman rulers tried several times to rename this month in honor of certain emperors or members of their families. But the people continued to call this month October.

Long ago, the people in England had their names for this month. One name was *Winmonath*, or "wine month," for this was the time of year they made wine. Another name was *Winterfylleth*, meaning "winter full moon." At that time, the people believed that winter began with the full moon in this month.

Nigeria celebrates

With a rat-a-tat-tat of drums and a blare of bugles, rows of soldiers march smartly down the street. Overhead, there is a roar as a formation of warplanes rushes through the sky. Later, there will be fireworks. It's National Day in Nigeria.

Nigeria is on the west coast of Africa. Until 1960, Nigeria was part of the British Commonwealth. Then, on October 1, 1960, Great Britain granted Nigeria its independence. Nigeria adopted a green and white flag—green representing agriculture and white symbolizing unity and peace.

October 1 is a national holiday that Nigerians celebrate with great joy.

Honor for a Viking

The Vikings were hardy, daring sea-farers
from what are now Norway, Denmark, and
Sweden. More than a thousand years ago,
some Norwegian Vikings under Eric the Red
ventured far out into the Atlantic Ocean.
They found a new land, which they named
Greenland.

According to the Viking sagas, or stories,
Leif Ericson, a son of Eric the Red, sailed
west from Greenland and found still another
new land. The land Leif Ericson found was
North America. No one knows exactly where
he landed, but scientists have discovered the
remains of a thousand-year old Viking village
in Newfoundland.

Many people feel that Leif Ericson was the
discoverer of America. In the United States,
October 9 is officially Leif Ericson Day. On
this day, Norwegian-Americans have special
dinners and ceremonies. These are to honor
Leif Ericson and the hardy Vikings who
found America nearly five hundred years
before Columbus.

The soldier from Poland

Count Casimir Pulaski was a Polish nobleman who fought for the Americans in the Revolutionary War.

While in France in 1777, Pulaski learned of the American Revolution from Benjamin Franklin. He decided to go to America and offer his services to General George Washington.

Pulaski was such an expert cavalryman—a soldier who fought on horseback—that Washington convinced Congress to make him a brigadier general. Pulaski then formed a cavalry corps called Pulaski's Legion. Pulaski fought bravely in a number of battles.

*Polish-Americans dance in
the street at a Pulaski Day
parade.*

In October 1779, the American army
attacked a British force holding the city of
Savannah, Georgia. Count Pulaski led a
cavalry charge against the British. The
charge failed and Pulaski was wounded. Two
days later, he died.

October 11, the date of Casimir Pulaski's
death, is now an official holiday in the United
States. Some cities, especially those where
many Polish-Americans live, have parades and
other celebrations on this day.

"Sail on!"

Behind him lay the gray Azores,
  Behind the Gates of Hercules;
Before him not the ghost of shores,
  Before him only shoreless seas.
The good mate said: "Now must we pray,
  For lo! the very stars are gone.
Brave Admiral, speak, what shall I say?"
  "Why, say, 'Sail on! sail on! and on!'"

from *Columbus*
by Joaquin Miller

Christopher Columbus was sure he could reach the Indies—Japan and China—by sailing west across the Atlantic Ocean. Others said no, it couldn't be done. Oh, they knew the world was round. That was not the problem. The real problem was distance.

Columbus thought that the Atlantic Ocean was very narrow. Others argued that the distance to Japan was four times greater than Columbus thought. And what no one knew was that there was a "New World" between Spain and Japan. But the king and queen of Spain gave Columbus the money and ships he needed. After all, the risk was small. And if Columbus was right, Spain would be rich.

Columbus sailed from Palos, Spain, on August 3, 1492. He took his three ships, the *Santa María*, the *Niña*, and the *Pinta*, south as far as the Canary Islands. He stayed there until September 6. Then he sailed westward. For more than a month, the ships moved through a seemingly endless sea. The frightened sailors demanded that Columbus turn back, but he insisted they must sail on.

Finally, on October 12, 1492, they saw land. Columbus thought he had reached the Indies—which is why he called the people Indians. But it was not Japan or China. It was part of a "New World." Columbus' voyage made America known to the people of Europe. This truly changed the world. It is why Columbus is honored.

In the United States, Columbus Day is celebrated on the second Monday of October. Because Columbus sailed under the Spanish flag, people in Spain also celebrate Columbus Day. But Columbus wasn't Spanish. He was Italian. He was born in Genoa, Italy, and so Italians also celebrate Columbus Day. People in many Central and South American countries honor Columbus on October 12, because he also discovered their lands.

The Festival of Lights

It is late autumn in India, the day before Divali, or the Festival of Lights. For many who practice the Hindu religion, Divali is the first day of the new year.

In many homes, the children are busy making special holiday lamps. They fill little clay bowls with mustard oil. Into the oil they put a little wick made of cotton. These lamps are a very important part of Divali. They are lit on the fourth day of this five-day festival. *Divali* means "row of lights."

While the children are making the Divali lamps, mothers and grandmothers are getting ready for the holiday, too. The walls and floor of the house are whitewashed, and garlands of flowers are hung over the door. Sweet cakes and candies are prepared.

The next day—Divali—everyone gets up early. The day is spent visiting relatives. There are lots of good things to eat, and gifts are exchanged. There may also be a visit to a street fair, where the children can go on rides and watch fireworks.

Before sunset, each family sets out its Divali lamps. These are placed in a row along the roof, on window sills, and on the road or street leading to the house. As the sky grows dark, the lamps are lit. All over the countryside the little lights glow, like stars brought down from the sky.

Hindu children know that these lights will

During the Festival of
Lights, many palaces and
other buildings in India
are outlined with strings
of electric lights.

help guide Lakshmi, the goddess of wealth
and good luck. She will fly down to earth on
the back of the Heavenly Swan and visit each
house where the lamps are twinkling. Then,
the family in that house will be blessed with
good luck for a whole year.

"Trick or treat"

What's that? It's a ghost! Look, there goes a witch!

There's no need to be afraid, though. All these ghosts, witches, and other strange creatures are only children in costumes. It's October 31, Halloween—and that's a special holiday for children in the United States. It is a time when they can dress up as ghosts, witches, monsters, animals, favorite athletes, or other people or things.

On the afternoon of Halloween, many schools allow younger children to wear their costumes to class. Some schools have Halloween parties and costume parades. There are often contests to pick the children with the best costumes.

Some children go out to trick or treat on Halloween. They go from door to door, ring doorbells, and call out, "Trick or treat!" People who answer the doors put treats into the children's bags.

In many towns and cities now, children do not go out to trick or treat. It is considered unsafe. Instead, towns, cities, and even neighborhoods have big parties for the children. Children who go to the parties get treats. They eat cakes and cookies that are decorated with Halloween colors, orange and black. They drink sweet apple cider and dunk for apples in tubs of water. They play games. They may even turn the lights down low and tell shivery stories about ghosts and monsters and witches and black cats. After all, that's what Halloween is all about!

Since most holidays honor famous people or celebrate important events, what started this rather strange holiday that seems to "honor" witches and ghosts?

Halloween wasn't always a children's "fun" holiday. At one time, it was a very serious and rather frightening event.

Thousands of years ago, in England, Scotland, Ireland, and some other places, the day that is now November 1 was the beginning of the new year. People also thought of this day as the start of winter. They called it "Summer's End."

People believed there was a sort of war between winter, with its cold and darkness, and summer, with its bright, long days and pleasant greenery. They felt that at Summer's End, the "army" of winter—ghosts, goblins, witches, and other evil creatures—grew very strong.

The night before Summer's End, October 31, became a frightening time. People were sure that all the wicked creatures would be out celebrating—and might attack them.

To protect themselves, people held special ceremonies. They built big bonfires on hilltops to light up the night. They put on masks and animal skins. They hoped that their strange "costumes" would keep the evil creatures from knowing who they were.

Hundreds of years later, the Christian religion came to these countries. November 1 became a Christian holiday known as All Saints' Day or All Hallows' Day. *Hallow* means "holy," and this was the day to honor all the

holy ones, or saints, especially those who had no days of their own.

The night before All Hallows' Day, October 31, became known as All Hallows' E'en (*e'en* is an old way of saying "evening"). After a time, it was shortened to Halloween.

Many people, especially in England, kept up some of the old Summer's End customs. Even after thousands of years had passed, people remembered that ghosts, goblins, and witches were supposed to be most powerful on Halloween. They also remembered that this was a night on which people had once put on special costumes.

This is why people in America and the British Isles think of Halloween as a time of ghosts and monsters, and it is why American children wear costumes on Halloween. October 31 was once a time of terror, but now it's just a night of spooky fun.

Make a jack-o'-lantern

For this project, ask a grown-up to do all the cutting and carving. After the top of the pumpkin is cut off, scoop the pulp out with a spoon. Save the top to use as a lid.

Next, draw on the eyes, nose, and mouth with a felt pen. These can be cut out, or just cut the skin and peel it off.

For ears, add leaves, small gourds, or halves of a green pepper. You can use a carrot or a red pepper for a nose. Hold these vegetables in place with toothpicks.

You can light your pumpkin with a candle or with a flashlight. Put the top back on and your jack-o'-lantern is ready.

November

1

Benvenuto Cellini (1500) Italian goldsmith and sculptor

Sholem Asch (1880) Polish-born author who wrote in Yiddish and English

2

James K. Polk (1795) 11th President of the United States

Warren G. Harding (1865) 29th President of the United States

3

Stephen Austin (1793) American pioneer in Texas

Vilhjalmur Stefansson (1879) Canadian author and Arctic explorer

4

Will Rogers (1879) American cowboy who became famous as a humorist and social critic

Art Carney (1918) American comedian and actor

Who shares my birthday?

Is your birthday in November? The names of some of the famous people born in November are shown on the calendar on this page and the next. What do you know about the person who shares your birthday?

5

Eugene V. Debs (1855) American labor leader

Will Durant (1885) American philosopher, educator, and historian

6

John Philip Sousa (1854) American bandmaster

Ignace Jan Paderewski (1860) Polish pianist, composer, and statesman

7

Marie Sklodowska Curie (1867) Polish-born physicist who won Nobel Prize for chemistry in 1911

Joan Sutherland (1926) Australian opera star

8

Margaret Mitchell (1900) American author of *Gone with the Wind*, a Civil War story

Katharine Hepburn (1909) American star of stage and movies

9

Benjamin Banneker (1731) American astronomer and mathematician

Florence Sabin (1871) American scientist and public health worker

10

Martin Luther (1483) German religious leader

Vachel Lindsay (1879) American poet

11

Fyodor Dostoevsky (1821) Russian author

Maude Adams (1872) American stage actress

12

Grace Kelly (1929) princess of Monaco and a former actress

Nadia Comaneci (1961) Romanian gold medal Olympic gymnast

13

James C. Maxwell (1831) Scottish physicist and teacher

Robert Louis Stevenson (1850) Scottish author of *Treasure Island*

14

Jawaharlal Nehru (1889) 1st prime minister of India

Edward White (1930) American astronaut; first man to walk in space

15

William Herschel (1738) English astronomer

Felix Frankfurter (1882) associate justice of the U.S. Supreme Court

16

Louis H. Fréchette (1839) Canadian writer of lyric poetry

W. C. Handy (1873) American songwriter and bandleader, known as "Father of the Blues"

17

Bernard Montgomery (1887) British general and field marshal in World War II

18

Louis Daguerre (1787) French inventor of the daguerreotype

Sir William S. Gilbert (1836) English songwriter

19

James A. Garfield (1831) 20th President of the United States

Indira Gandhi (1917) first woman prime minister of India

20

Alistair Cooke (1908) British-born author; host of "Masterpiece Theatre"

Maya Michailovna Plisetskaya (1925) Russian ballerina

21

Voltaire (1694) French author and philosopher; his real name was François Marie Arouet

William Beaumont (1785) American surgeon

22

Abigail Adams (1744) wife of President John Adams and mother of President John Quincy Adams

George Eliot (1819) English author

23

Franklin Pierce (1804) 14th President of the United States

Sir Gilbert Parker (1862) Canadian author of historical stories

24

Junípero Serra (1713) Spanish missionary who founded the first mission in California

Zachary Taylor (1784) 12th President of the United States

25

John XXIII (1881) Roman Catholic pope from 1958 to 1963 (born Angelo Roncalli)

Joe DiMaggio (1914) New York Yankee baseball star for 25 years

26

Mary E. Walker (1832) American Civil War doctor; won the Medal of Honor

Charles M. Schulz (1922) American cartoonist; creator of "Peanuts"

27

Chaim Weizmann (1874) Israeli statesman and 1st president of Israel

Charles A. Beard (1874) American historian and teacher

28

William Blake (1757) English poet and painter

Stefan Zweig (1881) Austrian author of stories, poems, and biographies

29

Andrés Bello (1781) Chilean poet

Louisa May Alcott (1832) American author of *Little Women* and other books

30

Jonathan Swift (1667) English author of *Gulliver's Travels*

Mark Twain (1835) American author (real name, Samuel Clemens)

The "ninth" month

November is the eleventh month of the year. It has thirty days. In ancient Roman times, when the year began in March, November was the ninth month of the year. This month got its name from *novem*, the Latin word for "nine."

When the Romans made January the first month of the year, November became the eleventh month. Tiberius, the second Roman emperor, was born in November. So, the Romans offered to rename the month in his honor. But Tiberius refused, and the month continued to be known as November.

Fierce, howling winds sweep over England at this time of year. So, one name the people living there long ago had for this month was *Wind-monath*, or "wind month."

During this month, animals were killed so as to have food for the winter. So, another name for this month was *Blod-monath*, or "blood month."

The Gunpowder Plot

"A penny for the Guy! A penny for the Guy!"

The merry shouts of children asking for money echo up and down the streets. And with them they have "the Guy," a straw dummy dressed in old clothes. Many of the children are wearing costumes and masks.

It is November 5, and people in England are celebrating a holiday called Guy Fawkes Day.

Nearly four hundred years ago, in 1605, a man named Guy Fawkes tried to blow up a government building. He wanted to kill King James I and the king's leaders. Fawkes was one of a group of men who felt that the government was treating Roman Catholics unfairly.

The king and his leaders were to meet on November 5. So, the group placed barrels of gunpowder in a cellar beneath the building where the king and others were to meet. Guy Fawkes was to light the fuse that would set off the explosion. But the plot was discovered before he had a chance to do this. The king was saved, and Guy Fawkes was hanged.

Ever since, Guy Fawkes Day has been a time for merrymaking. It is a holiday that both children and grown-ups enjoy. The best part comes as darkness falls. Then, straw dummies of Guy Fawkes are tossed onto huge bonfires. Amid cries of glee, firecrackers pop and "the Guy" goes up in a blaze of fire.

These college students are voting in an election. At the end of the day, the votes will be counted and the winners will be announced.

A day to vote

Election Day

For months, people have heard speeches on TV, seen signs and posters, and read the newspapers. Now, all across the United States, they are going to polling places to vote. It's Election Day.

Election Day is always the first Tuesday after the first Monday in November. In most election years, voters elect representatives and senators from their state to the United States government. They also elect officials in their own state, county, and town. And every four years, they elect a President of the United States.

Voting gives people a chance to decide how their government should be run. They can elect candidates who will work for the kind of government they want. Voting is so important that in many states Election Day is a holiday in years when a President is elected. In other states, people get time off from work to vote.

Lest we forget

In Flanders fields the poppies blow
Between the crosses, row on row,
That mark our place; and in the sky
The larks, still bravely singing, fly
Scarce heard amid the guns below.

from *In Flanders Fields*
by John McCrae

For more than four years the war raged on. Then, at 11:00 A.M. on November 11, 1918, the guns stopped firing. World War I was over—on the eleventh hour of the eleventh day of the eleventh month. The armistice—the agreement to end the war—had been signed.

November 11 became Armistice Day, a day on which many nations honor those who died for their country. In France and the United Kingdom, it is still called Armistice Day. In Canada, it is called Remembrance Day.

In 1954, in the United States, Armistice Day was changed to Veterans Day. It became a time to honor men and women who have served in the nation's armed forces.

Each year, at Arlington National Cemetery in Virginia, there are special ceremonies.

These begin with two minutes of silence, followed by a bugler playing taps. A wreath is placed at the Tomb of the Unknowns—the graves of three unknown Americans, one from World War I, one from World War II, and one from the Korean War.

On Remembrance Day in Canada, two children kneel for a moment to remember all the Canadians who died for their country.

In a ceremony in Washington, D.C., a wreath is placed at the Vietnam Veterans Memorial to honor Americans in the armed forces who died in the Vietnam War.

Japanese children and their mothers dress in their finest clothes when they go to a shrine to celebrate Shichi-Go-San.

Shichi-Go-San
November 15

Seven-five-three

In Japan, children who are three, five, or seven years old are thought to be especially fortunate. So, on November 15, families who have children of these ages take part in a very old festival.

This special children's festival is called *Shichi-Go-San*, or "Seven-Five-Three." It is for boys and girls who are three or five or seven years old.

On this day, the children dress in their finest clothes. Some wear Western-style clothes. Others follow the old customs. They wear their traditional kimonos, which are beautiful, brightly colored robes made of cotton or silk. And every child has a long,

narrow paper bag. On each colorfully decorated bag there are pictures, usually of a pine tree, a tortoise, and a crane. These are symbols of youth and long life.

When everyone is ready, the families go to a shrine, or place of worship. There, they give thanks for the good health of the children. They also ask for a blessing for the future health and happiness of the children.

Outside the shrine, there are stalls where the parents buy candy and toys to fill the children's paper bags. After the families return home, the children give some of their candy to visiting friends and relatives. In return, the children are often given gifts. Finally, the day may end with a party.

Truly *Shichi-Go-San* is a very special day for a child of three, or five, or seven!

On Shichi-Go-San, *the children get bags of candy. The symbols on the bags stand for youth and long life.*

Every Thanksgiving Day, there's a huge parade in New York City. It is put on by a big department store. The parade is famous for giant balloons of favorite comic and storybook characters such as Snoopy.

Thanksgiving Day

Harvest holiday

Mm-mmmm! Smell the turkey cooking! It's Thanksgiving Day and company's coming! In the United States and Canada, this is a special holiday. Families and friends gather to eat and give thanks for their blessings.

Thanksgiving Day is really a harvest festival. This is why it is celebrated in late fall, after the crops are in. But one of the first thanksgivings in America had nothing to do with a good harvest. On December 4, 1619, colonists from England landed near what is now Charles City, Virginia. They knelt down and thanked God for their safe journey across the Atlantic.

The first New England Thanksgiving did celebrate a plentiful harvest. The Pilgrims landed at what is now Plymouth, Massachusetts, in 1620. They had a difficult time, and the first winter was cruel. Many of the Pilgrims died. But the next year, in 1621, they had a good harvest. So, Governor Bradford declared a three-day feast.

The Pilgrims invited Indian friends to join them for the special feast. Everyone brought food. There was fish, deer meat (venison), turkey, and duck. Corn was crushed to make hot corn-meal bread and Indian pudding.

In time, other colonies began to celebrate a day of thanksgiving. But there was no national Thanksgiving Day.

During the Civil War, Sarah Josepha Hale, who wrote "Mary Had a Little Lamb," convinced Abraham Lincoln to do something about it. He proclaimed the last Thursday of November 1863 as a day of prayerful thanksgiving. Today, Americans celebrate this happy harvest festival on the fourth Thursday in November.

Canadians celebrate Thanksgiving Day in much the same way as their American neighbors. But the Canadian Thanksgiving Day falls on the second Monday in October.

Thanksgiving Day

by Lydia Maria Child

Over the river and through the wood,
  To Grandfather's house we go,
    The horse knows the way
    To carry the sleigh
Through the white and drifted snow.

Over the river and through the wood,
  Oh, how the wind does blow!
    It stings the toes,
    And bites the nose,
As over the ground we go.

Over the river and through the wood,
  To have a first-rate play,
    Hear the bells ring,
    "Ting-a-ling-ling!"
Hurrah for Thanksgiving Day!

Over the river and through the wood,
　Trot fast my dapple gray!
　　Spring over the ground,
　　Like a hunting hound!
For this is Thanksgiving Day.

Over the river and through the wood,
　And straight through the barnyard gate,
　　We seem to go
　　Extremely slow,
It is so hard to wait!

Over the river and through the wood—
　Now Grandmother's cap I spy!
　　Hurrah for the fun
　　Is the pudding done?
Hurrah for the pumpkin pie!

St. Andrew's Day
November 30

The First-Called

On the last day of November, Saint Andrew, the patron saint of Scotland and Greece, is honored in many parts of the world. Who was this man who is honored by so many different people?

Andrew was a simple fisherman. He lived with his brother Peter in Galilee. Then Jesus

Christ called Andrew to follow Him. Because Andrew was probably the first of the apostles, he is often spoken of as "The First-Called."

"I will make you fishers of men," Jesus said to Andrew and to Peter. So the two men put down their nets and followed Jesus.

Jesus commanded the apostles to "go into the world and preach the gospel to every creature." And this is what Andrew did. It is believed he preached in Greece. It is said that he even traveled into Russia.

But Andrew angered the Romans by preaching the word of Jesus Christ. Finally, the Romans crucified him on an X-shaped cross. This kind of cross is called the cross of Saint Andrew. You can see this white cross on the flags of Scotland and England.

It is said that some of Andrew's bones were later taken to Scotland for burial. The Scots not only made him their patron saint, they also remembered this humble man through the St. Andrew's Society.

There are St. Andrew's societies in almost every part of the world. These groups work to help the poor and the needy. And each year the groups hold great banquets on November 30, the feast day of Saint Andrew.

These affairs are very much like the ones held on Robbie Burns's birthday (see page 54). The main part of the dinner is, of course, that special Scottish dish called haggis. And throughout the evening, the swirl of bagpipes fills the air.

December

1

Woody Allen (1935) American comedian, actor, and filmmaker

Lee Trevino (1939) American professional golf champion

2

Georges Seurat (1859) French artist who started a way of painting called *pointillism*

Tracy Austin (1962) American tennis player

3

George McClellan (1826) Union general in the Civil War

Joseph Conrad (1857) Polish-born author who wrote some of the greatest novels in English

4

Thomas Carlyle (1795) Scottish author of essays and French and English history

Edith Cavell (1865) World War I English nurse

Who shares my birthday?

Is your birthday in December? The names of some of the famous people born in December are shown on the calendar on this page and the next. What do you know about the person who shares your birthday?

5

Martin Van Buren (1782) 8th President of the United States

Walt Disney (1901) American creator of Mickey Mouse and other movie cartoon characters

6

George Armstrong Custer (1838) American cavalry officer; defeated at Little Bighorn

Dave Brubeck (1920) American jazz composer and pianist

7

Rudolf Friml (1879) Austrian-born composer of operettas

Joyce Kilmer (1886) American poet; best known for "Trees"

8

Eli Whitney (1765) American inventor of the cotton gin

Padraic Colum (1881) Irish poet, playwright, and author of young people's books

9

John Milton (1608) English poet

Joel Chandler Harris (1848) American author of the Uncle Remus stories

10

César Franck (1822) Belgian composer of music for piano and orchestra

Emily Dickinson (1830) American poet

11

Hector Berlioz (1803) French composer, conductor, critic, and writer

Annie Jump Cannon (1863) American astronomer

12

John Jay (1745) American diplomat and 1st chief justice of the United States

Gustave Flaubert (1821) French author

13

Emily Carr (1871) Canadian painter and writer

Alvin York (1887) American hero in World War I

14

James Doolittle (1896) U.S. Air Force general

Margaret Chase Smith (1897) American senator from Maine

15

Maxwell Anderson (1888) American playwright and 1933 Pulitzer Prize winner

J. Paul Getty (1892) American billionaire

16

Jane Austen (1775) English author of *Pride and Prejudice* and other books

Margaret Mead (1901) American anthropologist and author

17

John Greenleaf Whittier (1807) American poet

Arthur Fiedler (1894) long-time conductor of the Boston Pops Orchestra

18

Charles Wesley (1707) English clergyman who wrote many hymns

Benjamin O. Davis, Jr. (1912) the first black U.S. major general

19

Albert Michelson (1852) first American physicist to win the Nobel Prize in physics (1907)

Cicely Tyson (1939) American actress

20

Maud Gonne (1865) advocate of Irish freedom

Harvey Firestone (1868) American founder of Firestone Tire & Rubber Company

21

Benjamin Disraeli (1804) twice prime minister of Great Britain

Albert Payson Terhune (1872) American author of stories about dogs

22

James Oglethorpe (1696) English founder and first governor of the colony of Georgia

Giacomo Puccini (1858) Italian opera composer who wrote *La Bohème*

23

Richard Arkwright (1732) British inventor of a machine to make thread

José Greco (1918) Italian-born Spanish dancer

24

Kit Carson (1809) American frontier scout

Matthew Arnold (1822) English poet and literary critic

25

Isaac Newton (1642) English mathematician who discovered the law of gravity

Clara Barton (1821) founder of the American Red Cross

26

Thomas Gray (1716) English poet; wrote "Elegy Written in a Country Churchyard"

George Dewey (1837) American admiral who took Manila in 1898

27

Johannes Kepler (1571) German astronomer

Louis Pasteur (1822) French scientist who discovered disease is spread by bacteria

28

Carol Ryrie Brink (1895) American author

Earl (Fatha) Hines (1905) American jazz musician

29

Andrew Johnson (1808) 17th President of the United States

Woodrow Wilson (1856) 28th President of the United States

30

Rudyard Kipling (1865) English author of *The Jungle Book, Just So Stories, Captains Courageous*, and other books

31

Henri Matisse (1869) French painter

Odetta (Felicious Gordon) (1930) American folk singer

The "tenth" month

December is the twelfth month of the year. It has thirty-one days. In ancient Roman times, when the year began in March, December was the tenth month of the year. This month got its name from *decem*, the Latin word for "ten."

When the Romans made January the first month of the year, December became the twelfth month. But it kept its old name.

In the northern half of the world, winter begins on December 21 or 22. There, it is the shortest day of the year. At the same time, summer begins in the southern half of the world. There, it is the longest day of the year.

People living in England long ago called this month *Winter-monath*, or "winter month." Later, many of the people became Christians. They called this month *Halig-monath*, or "holy month," because Christ was born on December 25.

**Feast of
Saint Nicholas**
December 6

Europe's Santa Claus

A long time ago, a bishop named Nicholas
lived in what is now the country of Turkey.
No one knows much about him. But there are
stories that he often helped children who
were in need.

Many years after his death, Nicholas was
made a saint. In time, he became the patron
saint of children. Today, the date of his death,
December 6, is an important holiday in some
countries in Europe. On the night before,
children put out their shoes or hang up their
stockings. Early next morning, they rush to
see what gifts Saint Nicholas left them.

Saint Nicholas visits towns and cities, leads
parades, talks to children, and often hands
out small gifts. He is dressed as a bishop, of

302

Sinterklaas, *as the Dutch call Saint Nicholas, arrives in the city of Amsterdam by boat. Today, he always has a number of helpers. Each helper is known as Black Peter. One of them has a book that contains the names of good and bad children.*

course, wearing a red or white robe and a tall, pointed hat.

Saint Nicholas always has a helper. In the Netherlands, this helper is called Black Peter. In Germany, he's *Knecht Ruprecht*. In parts of France, he's *Père Fouettard*. And in Luxembourg, he's known as *Hoesecker*.

Of course, all the children love Saint Nicholas. But they're quite afraid of his helper. For it is the helper who keeps track of who was good and who was naughty. Naughty children may get only switches, with which their parents can spank them! They may even be carried away in the helper's bag until they learn to be good!

Dutch settlers in America continued to celebrate this feast day. Their name for Saint Nicholas was *Sinterklaas*. And in English, this became Santa Claus.

Juan Diego's vision

On December 12 each year, thousands of people gather at a hill in Mexico City. They come from all over Mexico. Many have walked long distances to reach the shrine of Our Lady of Guadalupe.

The shrine is built on the spot where a poor Indian said he had seen a vision. About 450 years ago, the man, Juan Diego, was walking by the hill. Suddenly he saw the figure of a young Indian woman, surrounded by bright light. She had black hair, dark eyes, and a dark skin. She told him she was the mother of God, and the mother of all Indians. She told him she wanted a shrine built there.

Juan Diego told this story to a bishop. The bishop didn't believe him. But the Indian later returned and claimed to have seen the vision again. He told the bishop that roses had suddenly appeared on the hillside. The woman had told him to gather the roses in his cloak. When Juan Diego opened his cloak to show them to the bishop, the roses fell out. And on the cloak was a painting of the woman Juan Diego had seen.

Juan Diego told the bishop that the woman called herself Holy Mary of Guadalupe. The bishop finally decided that Juan Diego had seen the Virgin Mary, whom Christians believe is the mother of Jesus. He allowed a shrine to be built on the hill. The cloak with the painting on it now hangs in the shrine.

And Our Lady of Guadalupe is Mexico's
patron saint.

Everyone in Mexico celebrates Guadalupe
Day. It is the most important religious
holiday in Mexico. People put pictures and
statues of the Virgin of Guadalupe in their
windows. Gifts of flowers, pigs, chickens, and
eggs are brought to churches. And colorful
puppet shows re-enact the story of Juàn
Diego's vision.

*Each year on Guadalupe
Day, thousands of people
fill this great plaza in
Mexico City. They come
to visit the old and new
shrines built to honor
Mexico's patron saint,
Our Lady of Guadalupe.*

305

Cakes and candles

Down the village street comes a small group of young people. At the head of the group walks a pretty girl in a long, white dress. Upon her head she wears a crown of green leaves and seven glowing candles. In her hands she carries a tray of little cakes. Behind her walk some younger girls, also in white, carrying candles. A number of boys in tall, pointed hats follow them.

Processions such as this can be seen in all parts of Sweden on St. Lucia Day, December 13. The girls and boys bring cakes and coffee to homes, hospitals, factories, and offices.

The girl with the crown represents Saint Lucia, a young Christian girl. She was killed by Roman soldiers about fifteen hundred years ago for refusing to give up her religion.

Because Saint Lucia was an Italian, her day is also celebrated in Italy. There, people honor her with bonfires and parades on her feast day, December 13.

The happiest holiday

Away in a manger,
No crib for a bed,
The little Lord Jesus
Lay down His sweet head;

The stars in the bright sky
Looked down where He lay—
The little Lord Jesus
Asleep on the hay.

from *A Little Children's Book
for Schools and Families*

For Christians all over the world, Christmas is an important, happy holiday. It is the day that celebrates the birth of Jesus Christ, about two thousand years ago. *Christmas* is a short form of *Christ's Mass*, an old name for this day. It means a mass, or church service, in honor of Christ.

The story of Christmas comes from the Bible. Here is the way it is told by Saint Luke:

And she brought forth her firstborn son, and wrapped him in swaddling clothes, and laid him in a manger; because there was no room for them in the inn.

And there were in the same country shepherds abiding in the field, keeping watch over their flock by night. And, lo, the angel of the Lord came upon them, and the glory of the Lord shone round about them; and they were sore afraid. And the angel said unto them,

"Fear not: for, behold, I bring you good tidings of great joy, which shall be to all people. For unto you is born this day in the city of David a Saviour, which is Christ the Lord. And this shall be a sign unto you; ye shall find the babe wrapped in swaddling clothes, lying in a manger."

A crèche is a model of the stable where Christ was born. This French crèche includes a number of figures that stand for townspeople who would like to have taken part in the first Christmas at Bethlehem.

Many Christmas customs are based on the birth of Christ. People give each other presents because the Three Wise Men, or Three Kings, brought presents to the baby Jesus. Christians sing songs, called carols, that tell about Christ's birth. And they put up scenes of Jesus' birth, with figures of shepherds, the Three Kings, and animals around the tiny baby.

But some of the ways people celebrate Christmas have nothing to do with Christ's birthday. Many bits of older holidays have crept into Christmas!

It wasn't until about two hundred years

after Christ's time that Christians even thought about celebrating His birthday. No one knows the exact date of Christ's birth. December 25 may have been picked so as to turn people away from other holidays celebrated about this time of year.

The Romans had a holiday called Saturnalia that was celebrated in December. It was a time of gaiety, feasting, and parties. And in northern Europe there was a holiday known as Yule. People made great fires with huge logs. Then they danced around the fires, yelling. This was done to call back the sun and bring an end to winter.

In time, Christmas did take the place of such holidays as Yule and Saturnalia. But people kept some of the old customs—such as burning a Yule log and having feasts and parties. The word *Yule* is still used as a name for the Christmas season.

As time went on, new customs crept into Christmas, too. One of these was the Christmas tree. The idea of bringing a fir tree into the house may have started in Germany. Germans who moved to other lands took the idea with them, and people liked it.

Christmas is a special time for many children—the day they get presents left by a magical person. But in some countries, children get their gifts on December 6 (see page 302) or on January 6 (see page 48).

In the United States and Canada, presents are brought by Santa Claus. He drives through the sky in a sleigh drawn by eight

Xmas

Do you know why people sometimes write *Xmas* instead of Christmas? The custom goes back to the early Christians, who often wrote in Greek. In the Greek language, *X* is the first letter in *Christ*. So, *X* was often used as a holy symbol.

These Christmas shoppers in London, England, are going home with fresh holly and a pine-scented Christmas tree.

reindeer. He slips down the chimney, leaves gifts, and is on his way again. Santa Claus wears red clothes trimmed with white fur, and has a snow-white beard and mustache.

In England, the gift bringer is called Father Christmas. He looks much like Santa Claus, but he has a longer coat and a longer beard. In France, he's known as *Père Noël*. In Brazil, he's called *Papa Noël*.

In Germany, children get presents from *Christkindl*, the Christ child. And in Costa Rica, Colombia, and parts of Mexico, the gift bringer is *el Niño Jesus*, "the Infant Jesus."

In Sweden, gifts and goodies are brought by an elf called a *tomte*. He's a Christmas gnome who has a sleigh that is pulled by two goats.

The tomte *brings Christmas gifts in Sweden. He has a small sleigh pulled by goats.*

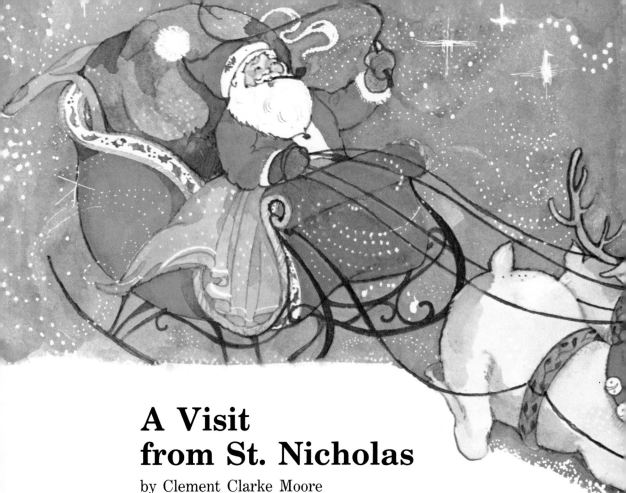

A Visit
from St. Nicholas

by Clement Clarke Moore

'Twas the night before Christmas, when all through
   the house
Not a creature was stirring, not even a mouse;
The stockings were hung by the chimney with care,
In hopes that St. Nicholas soon would be there;

The children were nestled all snug in their beds,
While visions of sugar-plums danced in their heads;
And mamma in her 'kerchief, and I in my cap,
Had just settled our brains for a long winter's nap,
When out on the lawn there arose such a clatter,
I sprang from the bed to see what was the matter.
Away to the window I flew like a flash,
Tore open the shutters and threw up the sash.

The moon on the breast of the new-fallen snow
Gave the luster of mid-day to objects below,
When, what to my wondering eyes should appear,
But a miniature sleigh, and eight tiny reindeer,
With a little old driver, so lively and quick,
I knew in a moment it must be St. Nick.

More rapid than eagles his coursers they came,
And he whistled, and shouted, and called them by name:
"Now, Dasher! now, Dancer! now, Prancer and Vixen!
On, Comet! on, Cupid! on, Donder and Blitzen!
To the top of the porch! to the top of the wall!
Now dash away! dash away! dash away all!"

As dry leaves that before the wild hurricane fly,
When they meet with an obstacle, mount to the sky,
So up to the house-top the coursers they flew,

With the sleigh full of toys, and St. Nicholas too.
And then, in a twinkling, I heard on the roof
The prancing and pawing of each little hoof.

As I drew in my head, and was turning around,
Down the chimney St. Nicholas came with a bound.
He was dressed all in fur, from his head to his foot,
And his clothes were all tarnished with ashes
   and soot;
A bundle of toys he had flung on his back,
And he looked like a peddler just opening his pack.

His eyes—how they twinkled! his dimples how merry!
His cheeks were like roses, his nose like a cherry!
His droll little mouth was drawn up like a bow,
And the beard of his chin was as white as the snow;
The stump of a pipe he held tight in his teeth,
And the smoke it encircled his head like a wreath;

He had a broad face and a little round belly,
That shook, when he laughed, like a bowlful of jelly.
He was chubby and plump, a right jolly old elf,
And I laughed when I saw him, in spite of myself;
A wink of his eye and a twist of his head,
Soon gave me to know I had nothing to dread;

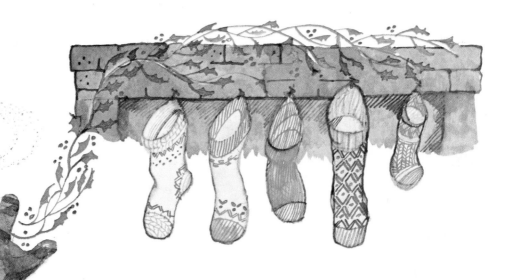

He spoke not a word, but went straight to his work,
And filled all the stockings; then turned with a jerk,
And laying his finger aside of his nose,
And giving a nod, up the chimney he rose;

He sprang to his sleigh, to his team gave a whistle,
And away they all flew like the down of a thistle.
But I heard him exclaim, ere he drove out of sight,
"Happy Christmas to all, and to all a good-night."

Hanukkah

The Feast of Lights

On the stove, crisp potato pancakes sputter in a skillet. In a corner, children spin square tops on the floor. On the table, candles twinkle in a candleholder. It's Hanukkah (HAH nu kah), the Jewish Feast of Lights.

Hanukkah is celebrated for eight days. It starts on the eve of the 25th day of the Hebrew month of Kislev, which falls in November or December. *Hanukkah* means "dedication." It is a festival in honor of a marvelous event that happened more than two thousand years ago.

At that time, the land of Israel was ruled by the Syrians. The Syrians had forbidden the

On the fifth night of Hanukkah, five of the candles on the menorah, or candleholder, are lighted. On this night, children are given coins and other gifts.

Jews to practice their religion. For three years, an army of Jewish rebels fought to free their land. In a great victory, they managed to recapture Jerusalem, the most important city of Israel.

The Jews then began special ceremonies to make the great Temple of Jerusalem holy again. One of the things they had to do was relight the Temple lamp. This lamp was supposed to burn at all times. But only a special oil, blessed by the priests, could be burned in the lamp.

The Jewish leaders found only a tiny jar of the special oil—just about enough to keep the lamp going for one day. It would take eight days to get more oil prepared. Rather than wait, they lit the lamp. They were amazed when the lamp burned steadily for eight days, until the new oil was ready.

The eight days of Hanukkah are in memory of the eight days the lamp stayed lit. A special symbol of Hanukkah is an eight-branched candlestick called a menorah (muh NAWR uh). On each day of Hanukkah, the candles are lit—one on the first day, two on the second day, and so on until, on the eighth day, all eight candles glow. A ninth candle, called the shammash, or "servant," is used to light the other candles. Some menorahs have a ninth branch to hold the shammash.

Hanukkah is a cheerful time. There may be a party to which friends and relatives are invited. A special Hanukkah food is potato pancakes, called *latkes*. Children often receive coins and other gifts.

Each evening, after the candles are lit, the family may sing songs and play games. Some games are played with a special Hanukkah toy—a square top called a dreidel (DRAY duhl). On each of the four sides of a dreidel there is a Hebrew letter. The letters stand for the words *Ness gadol haya sham*, which means "A great miracle happened there."

Twirl about, dance about,
    spin, spin, spin!
Turn, Dreidel, turn—
    Time to begin!

Soon it is Hanukkah—
    Fast, Dreidel, fast!
For you will lie still
    When Hanukkah's past.

Dreidel Song
by Efraim Rosenzweig

Potato Pancakes All Around

by Marilyn Hirsh

On a cold winter afternoon, Samuel the peddler walked down the road to a village.

He passed children sliding and sledding and skating.

"The children are out of school early," he said to himself, "because tonight is the first night of Hanukkah."

When Samuel reached the village, it was almost dark. He knocked on the door of a house. Mama opened the door and smiled at the peddler.

"A guest is always welcome," she said. "Come in. We are just lighting the first candle."

So they all sang the blessings together.

The two grandmothers went to the stove.

"Aha," thought Samuel, "now they'll start making potato pancakes."

"We'll use my recipe," Grandma Yetta said firmly.

"No, mine is better!" answered Grandma Sophie.

"Who needs recipes?" said Samuel the peddler. "I'll show you how to make potato pancakes from a crust of bread!"

"Some say for potato pancakes a pickle, a fish, or a cabbage is good," Samuel continued, "but I say a crust of bread is best."

"Ridiculous," said Grandma Yetta.

Potato pancakes, called *latkes* in Yiddish, are a favorite Hanukkah food.

319

"That's crazy," said Grandma Sophie.

"We're hungry!" cried the twins.

"So let's try the peddler's idea," said Mama.

Samuel took a bowl from his sack. "Who wants to hold it?" he asked.

"We do!" yelled the twins.

Samuel carefully grated a crust of bread into the bowl. "It looks delicious," he announced. "But it needs a little water."

The grandmothers wouldn't even look.

The peddler tasted the batter. "Some would say it needs salt . . . a little pepper, perhaps?"

"Even I know it needs salt and pepper," said Papa.

"Well, if you insist, I wouldn't say no," replied the peddler. And he added salt and pepper.

Samuel noticed a chicken looking in the window. "I think this chicken is trying to tell me something. But what could a chicken say?"

"I know!" cried Rachel. "The chicken is telling you to add eggs."

"I have heard of that," agreed the peddler. And he added six eggs.

"He takes advice from chickens," said Grandma Yetta.

"Do *you* have any suggestions?" he asked her politely.

"May you grow like an onion with your head in the ground!" she shouted.

"Ah, onions! A good idea," said Samuel.

So David hurried to chop some onions.

Samuel smiled. "Any minute now, we'll have potato pancakes."

"But what about the potatoes?" asked Sarah. "I grated all these potatoes, all by myself."

"It's not in my recipe," said Samuel, "but it's a sin to waste food. So what can it hurt? I'll add your potatoes."

And he did.

"What will you fry the potato pancakes in?" asked Grandma Yetta and Grandma Sophie at the same time.

"In a frying pan," answered Samuel. And he took one from his sack.

"Chicken fat is best," insisted Grandma Yetta.

"You may be right," said Samuel.

"Goose fat is better," declared Grandma Sophie.

"I wouldn't say no," Samuel replied.

So Samuel took a big spoonful of chicken fat and a big spoonful of goose fat and began to fry the potato cakes. Delicious smells filled the house.

Samuel kept on frying. More and more potato pancakes piled up.

Finally, it was time to eat. So they ate and ate and ate potato pancakes all around. Even

Grandma Yetta and Grandma Sophie agreed
that the potato pancakes were the best ever.

And they danced.

And they sang.

And they played games until very late.

Grandma Yetta and Grandma Sophie gave
the children pennies.

Then everyone went to sleep.

The next morning, the family begged
Samuel to stay for the whole eight days of
Hanukkah.

"Thank you," said Samuel, "but a peddler
must move along. I know you'll have a happy
Hanukkah . . . now that you can make potato
pancakes from a crust of bread."

A new holiday

From December 26 to January 1, many blacks in the United States celebrate a special time called Kwanzaa. Kwanzaa is their very own holiday—a way of honoring the customs of Africa, where their ancestors came from.

Kwanzaa is a new American holiday. But it is based on some very old African holidays. The word *kwanza* means "first" in the Swahili language of Africa. It was picked as the name for the new holiday because many African tribes celebrated the first harvest of their crops each year.

On the last night of Kwanzaa, all seven of the candles in the kinara, or candleholder, are lighted.

324

The spelling was changed from kwanza to Kwanzaa for two reasons. With the new spelling, there are seven letters—one for each day of the celebration. Also, it shows that this new holiday is not the same as the old African one.

Families celebrating Kwanzaa decorate their homes with straw mats, ears of corn, and a candleholder called a kinara. The straw mats stand for tradition. The ears of corn stand for the children. And the kinara stands for the family's African ancestors. The kinara holds seven candles, one for each day of Kwanzaa. Each day has special meaning, and a new candle is lit each day.

Each evening during Kwanzaa, the family lights the candle for that day. The children and their parents talk about the special meaning of that day. They may also exchange gifts. But the gifts can't be things that have been bought. They must be homemade—such as clothes made by the mother, toys made by the father, beads and bracelets made by the children.

Often, many families meet in a home or community center to celebrate each day of Kwanzaa together. On the last day, there is a feast, called a karamu, with music and dancing.

Kwanzaa was started in 1966 by an African-American professor and black cultural leader named M. Ron Karenga. In communities where many black Americans live, it has become a very important holiday.

Books to Read

If you enjoyed reading about holidays and birthdays in this book, you can read more about celebrations. Some books about them are listed here. Your school or your public library will have many others.

Ages 5 to 8

Arthur's Thanksgiving by Marc Brown (Little, Brown, 1983)
In this very funny book, Arthur is director of the Thanksgiving play. But he can't find anyone to play the turkey. He has a big surprise at the end of the book.

Fourth of July by Barbara M. Joose (Knopf, 1985)
Ross, who is five years old, is too young to do many things that are fun. But he gets the important job of helping to carry the banner in the Fourth of July parade.

Halloween ABC by Eve Merriam (Macmillan, 1987)
This book contains a Halloween poem for every letter of the alphabet.

Happy Birthday, Moon by Frank Asch (Simon and Schuster, 1982)
In this easy book, a little bear finds out that the moon shares his birthday. He buys a present for the moon.

The Hit of the Party by Franz Brandenberg (Greenwillow, 1985)
Jim's first surprise is finding out that his hamster has escaped. After he finds it, he goes to a costume party, where he gets another big surprise. Illustrations in this book were done by Aliki.

January Brings the Snow: A Seasonal Hide-and-Seek by Sara Coleridge (Franklin Watts, 1989)
This beautiful book, illustrated by Elizabeth Falconer, is based on Sara Coleridge's poem. A picture story is concealed under movable flaps.

Lion Dancer: Ernie Wan's Chinese New Year by Kate Waters and Madeline Slovenz-Low (Scholastic, 1990)
Ernie Wan tells about his family and their Chinese New Year celebration.

A Medieval Feast by Aliki (Crowell, 1983)
The king is coming to visit the Lord and Lady of Camdenton Manor. See and read about how they spend weeks preparing for the visit.

Merry Christmas, Ernest and Celestine by Gabrielle Vincent (William Morrow, 1984)
In this picture book, Ernest the bear and Celestine the mouse plan a party. Even though they have no money to buy the things they need, things somehow work out in the end.

The Polar Express by Chris Van Allsburg (Houghton Mifflin, 1985)
Late on Christmas Eve, a boy boards the Polar Express to go to the North Pole. There he gets a special gift from Santa that brings him joy throughout his life.

St. Patrick's Day by Joyce K. Kessel (Carolrhoda Books, 1982)
This is the story of St. Patrick and the holiday that honors him. Other books by the author include **Squanto and the First Thanksgiving** (1986), **Halloween** (1987), and **Valentine's Day** (1988).

Thanksgiving at the Tappletons' by
Eileen Spinelli (Harper & Row, 1982)
The relatives gather at the Tappletons'
house for Thanksgiving dinner. Despite
several mishaps, they have a meaningful,
although surprising, Thanksgiving.

Ages 9 to 12

Candles, Cakes, and Donkey Tails by
Lila Perl (Clarion, 1984)
How did birthdays begin? Why do people
in other countries have special birthday
customs? What do birthday symbols
mean? You can find the answers to these
questions and many more in this
book.

Celebrations by Myra Cohn Livingston
(Holiday House, 1985)
Poems about holidays, from New Year's
Eve to Christmas Eve, are accompanied
by Leonard Everett Fisher's beautiful
paintings.

Chinese New Year by Tricia Brown
(Henry Holt, 1987)
Gung Hay Fat Choy! That's what you'll
hear everywhere in Chinatown during
the Chinese New Year. Read all about
the customs and celebrations in this
colorfully illustrated book.

**The Christmas Fox and Other Winter
Poems** by John Bush (Dial, 1989)
A sly fox, dressed as Father Christmas,
is just one of the animal characters
featured in this book of poems.
Illustrations are watercolors by Peter
Weevers.

The Folklore of American Holidays
edited by Hennig Cohen and Tristram
Potter Coffin (Gale, 1987)
This book presents the folklore behind
customs, festivals, and holidays in
America throughout the year. Also
included are some songs, recipes for
traditional dishes, and other items of
interest.

Halloween Stories and Poems edited by
Caroline Feller Bauer (Lippincott,
1989)
Check in your closet, behind the door,
and under your bed before you read this
fun, spooky book.

Hanukkah: The Festival of Lights by
Jenny Koralek (Lothrop, Lee &
Shepard, 1990)
This is a sensitive telling of the story of
Hanukkah, complete with beautiful
illustrations by Juan Wijngaard.

Haunts and Taunts by Jean Chapman
(Childrens, 1983)
This book contains Halloween stories,
poems, and activities from around the
world.

Holidays by Bernice Burnett (Franklin
Watts, 1983)
People all over the world celebrate
holidays. Some holidays are different
from those you celebrate. Some that are
the same, such as New Year's Day, are
celebrated in a different way.

The Medieval Baker's Daughter by
Madeleine Pelner Cosman (Bard Hall,
1984)
This is an adventure in medieval life,
complete with costumes, banners, music,
food, and a mystery play.

Illustration acknowledgments

The publishers of *Childcraft* gratefully acknowledge the courtesy of the following photographers, agencies, and organizations for illustrations in this volume. When all the illustrations for a sequence of pages are from a single source, the inclusive page numbers are given. In all other instances, the page numbers refer to facing pages, which are considered as a single unit or spread. The words *"(left),"* *"(center),"* *"(top),"* *"(bottom),"* and *"(right)"* indicate position on the spread. All illustrations are the exclusive property of the publishers of *Childcraft* unless names are marked with an asterisk (*).

1:	*(top left)* Janet Palmer; *(top right)* Gwen Connelly; *(center right and bottom left)* Childcraft photo by Gilbert Meyers; *(bottom center)* Gwen Connelly; *(bottom right)* Orion Press *
2-9:	Gwen Connelly
10-11:	Dale Paysen
12-13:	Howard Post
14-17:	Gwen Connelly
18-19:	Howard Post
20-25:	Dale Paysen
26-29:	Gwen Connelly
30-33:	Angela Adams
34-35:	Gwen Connelly
36-37:	Roberta Polfus; Tournament of Roses *
38-39:	Gwen Connelly
40-47:	Marc Brown
48-49:	Michael A. Vaccaro, Louis Mercier *; Roberta Polfus
50-53:	Janet Palmer
54-55:	Gwen Connelly
56-57:	© Robert Frerck *
58-61:	Gwen Connelly
62-65:	Angela Adams
66-67:	Photri from Marilyn Gartman *
68-69:	Jon Goodell; Roberta Polfus; Russ Kinne, Photo Researchers *
70-73:	Jon Goodell
74-75:	Jon Goodell; Janet Palmer
76-77:	*Childcraft* photo
78-79:	Roberta Polfus; Lucinda McQueen
80-83:	Lucinda McQueen
84-85:	Janet Palmer; *Childcraft* photo
86-87:	J & M Ibbotson, Alaska Photo *; Roberta Polfus
88-89:	Jon Goodell
90-91:	Fred J. Maroon, Louis Mercier *
92-93:	Jon Goodell; Claus Meyer, Black Star *; © Peter Menzel *
94-95:	Jon Goodell
96-97:	Roberta Polfus
98-101:	Angela Adams
102-103:	Marc Brown
104-105:	Orion Press *; Roberta Polfus
106-107:	Australian Picture Library *; Marc Brown
108-109:	*Childcraft* photo by Jim Anderson
110-123:	Gwen Connelly
124-125:	© A.G.E. *
126-129:	Marc Brown
130-131:	*Childcraft* photo
132-133:	Angela Adams, adapted from *Misty of Chincoteague* by Marguerite Henry. Illustrated by Wesley Dennis. © 1947, 1975 by Rand McNally & Company
134-135:	Angela Adams
136-137:	Gwen Connelly
138-139:	Roberta Polfus; *Childcraft* photo by Tomokazu Imai
140-141:	Janet Palmer
142-143:	Gwen Connelly; *Childcraft* photo by Gilbert Meyers
144-145:	© James Sugar, Woodfin Camp & Associates *; Gwen Connelly
146-147:	*Childcraft* photo; Roberta Polfus
148-153:	Gwen Connelly

Index

This index is an alphabetical list of the important topics covered in this book. It will help you find information given in both words *and* pictures. To help you understand what an entry means, there is often a helping word in parentheses, for example, **Buddhism** (religion). If there is information in both words and pictures, you will see the words *(with pictures)* after the page number. If there is *only a* picture, you will see the word *(picture)* after the page number. If you do not find what you want in this index, please go to the General Index in Volume 15, which is a key to all of the books.

336